TANJA JONES

HOPE MCMATH

AARON DE GROFT

MAARTEN VAN DE **GUCHTE**

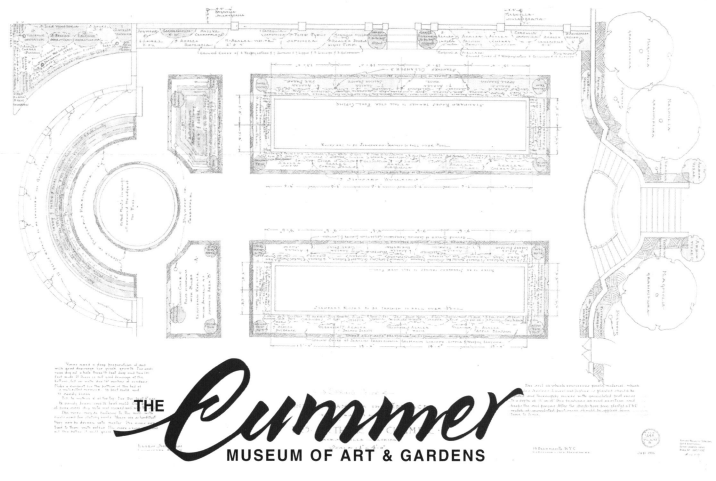

THE *Cummer*
MUSEUM OF ART & GARDENS

JACKSONVILLE, FLORIDA

NINAH·MAY·HOLDEN·CUMMER

EX LIBRIS

This publication was made possible by the Frances B. Barnett Charitable Trust

FOREWORD

The core of every art museum is its permanent collection. No matter how innovative, extensive, and successful a museum's exhibitions, outreach programs, and educational activities, the institution is ultimately evaluated on the basis of its artistic holdings. Catalogues of the permanent collection help ensure that knowledge of the collection reaches a wide audience. The museum's first handbook, published in 1961, celebrated the opening of the new building. Subsequent acquisitions were documented in catalogues published in 1965 and 1976. In the ensuing quarter century, museum visitors and colleagues from other institutions have been asking for an updated reference book of the collection. On the eve of the museum's fortieth anniversary, we are proud to present this publication of one hundred representative works of art from the permanent collection of the Cummer Museum of Art & Gardens.

From Ninah Cummer's relatively small collection of sixty pieces that launched the museum, the Cummer's permanent collection has grown to over five thousand works of art. This enormous growth was accomplished in no small part through the generosity of numerous patrons whose gifts of art ranged from single pieces to entire collections. Other notable acquisitions were purchased with endowments established for that purpose by benefactors and the Cummer Council. I encourage readers to note the credit line included with each entry that acknowledges these extraordinary gifts. To everyone associated with the creation of the Cummer's superb permanent collection go the thanks of the museum staff that now proudly oversees it.

The preparation of the handbook of the collection was an exciting and demanding project, executed with admirable verve and knowledge by Tanja Jones, Curator of Education, Hope McMath, Acting Director of Education, Aaron De Groft, Ph.D., Curator of Art, and Maarten van de Guchte, Ph.D., Associate Director & Chief Curator. Their task was to write brief, accessible, and informative entries on each of the works of art selected for this publication. They were aided by Jeannie Theriault who edited the text for the catalogue in an able and efficient manner. Jennifer Lisella, Registrar, provided crucial information on accessions and related matters. I would like to thank these staff members for their time and effort, and in particular Maarten van de Guchte who was the guiding force behind this project. They based their research in part on archival materials and notes prepared by previous staff members, docents, librarians, and other volunteers and colleagues. To this entire group, too large to be thanked individually, I extend the museum's gratitude. I would also like to thank Superstock, Inc., Jacksonville for providing the superb photographs. Graphic design was entrusted to Kym Staiff, DOC design consulting, St-Saphorin, Switzerland. The book was printed at Stamperia Artistica Nazionale in Turin, Italy.

I would like to express my deepest appreciation for the financial support of the Frances B. Barnett Charitable Trust that underwrote this publication. The longstanding friendship between the Barnett family and the museum is an inspiration to us all. This handsome and welcome addition to the Cummer literature would not have been possible without their generous support and enthusiasm.

And finally, on behalf of the entire staff, I would like to acknowledge our trustees, past and present, who wisely and diligently created an art museum that today is the pride of Jacksonville and all of northeast Florida. This handbook is a tribute to them for overseeing the evolution of this institution from the initial vision of Mrs. Cummer to the celebrated twenty-first century art and education center it has become.

Kahren Jones Arbitman, Ph.D.
Director

Cover: William-Adolphe Bouguereau, *Return from the Harvest* (detail), pl. 50
pg. 2 *Ex-Libris,* for Nina May Holden Cummer
pg. 9 *The Italian Garden*, 2000 (photographed by Thomas Hager)
pg. 117 *The Cummer Oak*, 2000 (photographed by Thomas Hager)
pg. 191 Ellen Biddle Shipman, *Planting Plan for the Terrace on the Estate of Mrs. Arthur Cummer*, File 248, Plan 8, Sept. 1931; Ellen Biddle Shipman Collection, Courtesy of the Division of Rare and Manuscript Collections, Cornell University Library

All measurements are given in inches; height precedes width precedes depth.

TABLE OF CONTENTS

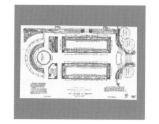

HISTORY OF THE CUMMER MUSEUM OF ART & GARDENS

The Cummer Museum of Art & Gardens, built on the site of the home of Arthur and Ninah Cummer, opened its doors November 10, 1961. The museum was the culmination of this couple's remarkable civic, social, and business involvement in northeast Florida.
Arthur Gerrish Cummer, originally from Morley, Michigan, was born in 1873 into a family of lumbermen. By the 1890s, the family business had spread from Michigan to Virginia and Florida. While attending the University of Michigan, Arthur met Ninah May Holden, a young woman from Michigan City, Indiana. Miss Holden, born October 16, 1875, was one of the few women attending the university. She received her undergraduate degree in 1895 and two years later, Arthur and Ninah were married. Immediately after their marriage, the couple moved to Jacksonville, Florida, then the center of the family's thriving lumber business.

Mrs. Cummer gave birth to a daughter on November 13, 1909. The girl was named DeEtte Holden Cummer, but sadly lived only seventeen days. Upon the death of their only child, the Cummers devoted themselves to civic and charitable work. Mr. Cummer, who had become president of the Cummer Lumber Company upon his father's death in 1909, served as director and vice president of Barnett National Bank and was a leading member of the Jacksonville Chamber of Commerce. Mrs. Cummer distinguished herself by organizing relief after the Jacksonville fire of 1901 and as a Red Cross volunteer during World War I. In 1910 she was elected president of the Women's Advisory Board of the Children's Home Society of Florida, a position she held until 1940. She organized the first Garden Club of Jacksonville in 1922 and was offered the presidency of the Garden Clubs of America, but declined the honor.

Mrs. Cummer had a keen interest in art, and purchased her first painting in 1906. This was the beginning of a collection that would eventually number more than sixty works and include paintings by Agnolo Gaddi, Peter Paul Rubens, Winslow Homer, and James McNeill Whistler. Upon Mr. Cummer's death in 1943, Mrs. Cummer began collecting art seriously. When she died on May 25, 1958, Mrs. Cummer's will established the DeEtte Holden Cummer Museum Foundation and bequeathed the bulk of her estate, including all the works of art, antiques, and the house itself to the foundation for the creation of an art museum. She understood that her fortune alone could not sustain a museum indefinitely. She stated that, "Naturally no civic undertaking can function adequately without the interest and support of the community within which it is located. Therefore it is hoped that there may be additions to the Foundation from time to time so that this Museum may rank favorably with those established in other cities in the United States during the last few decades."

The Cummer residence did not prove suitable for a museum and the architect Harold Saxelbye (1885–1964) was chosen to design a new museum building. Its exterior is special pink-toned Georgia brick with Indiana limestone trim and granite steps. The interior courtyard features a covered walk roofed with clay tiles from the original Cummer home. A period room in Tudor style within the museum preserves the atmosphere of the original Cummer residence. In 1991 the existing museum building was enlarged with the addition of two galleries on its east side facing the gardens. An adjunct building was purchased in 1990 to house the increasingly important art education center called *Art Connections*. Two acres of formal historic gardens surround and enhance the museum campus. Important gifts have enriched the Cummer Foundation in the last few decades. Particularly noteworthy additions are the Wark Collection of early Meissen porcelain, the Dennis C. Hayes Collection of Japanese woodblock prints, and the Eugène Louis Charvot Collection of nineteenth-century prints and paintings.

The Cummer Oak in the Cummer Gardens, c. 1945

The first garden at the Cummer residence was planted in 1903 and followed an English style. Wisteria, Rêve d'Or roses, and agapantha lilies abounded in this garden. Its aspect changed dramatically around 1925. Mrs. Cummer had heard a lecture by noted botanist Dr. H. Harold Hume about the beauty of the azalea, a flower not yet known in Florida horticultural circles. Intrigued by Dr. Hume's descriptions, Mrs. Cummer traveled to Charleston Gardens to see the azaleas in bloom. Delighted with this discovery, she returned to plant hundreds of these new flowers, which have since transformed Florida's gardens and parks. At the heart of the symmetrically arranged English or Azalea Garden is a small fountain, featuring in its center a sculpture of two young boys holding a goose.

The inspiration for the Italian Garden came from a trip Mrs. Cummer made to Italy. Among the various monuments, museums, and estates she visited, the garden at the Villa Gamberaia near Florence captured her imagination. Known for its Anglo-Italian design and distinct arches, this garden greatly impressed Mrs. Cummer. In 1931 she asked Ellen Biddle Shipman (1869–1950), known as "the dean of American women landscape architects," to design a garden for her. Shipman, familiar with the garden at Villa Gamberaia, created the Italian Garden. It is considered a signature piece in Shipman's oeuvre of residential gardens. Her garden designs are known for their axial plans, the integration of architectural elements, and the exquisite coloring and lushness of plantings. The Cummer Italian Garden is characterized by strong symmetry and quiet elegance. A series of arches covered with creeping fig direct the visitor's gaze through the gardens and over its ponds toward the St. Johns River.

The Italian Garden is one of the few Shipman gardens still in existence. Of particular interest to historians of landscape architecture are the original plans for the garden, which are kept in the Cornell University archives. The Cummer archives contain the complete list of plants ordered by Mrs. Cummer for her Italian Garden. Based on these invaluable records, a recent restoration has returned the garden to its original splendor.

Complementing the Cummer's English and Italian Gardens is the North Garden. This garden was designed in 1931 by the nationally known firm of Frederick Law Olmsted (1822–1903), best known for his design of Central Park in New York. Plans are being formulated to restore this garden. An invaluable help in the restoration of the North Garden will be the plans and notes of the Olmsted firm that are kept in the Manuscripts Division of the Library of Congress in Washington, D.C.

Above: *The Reflecting Pond* in the Cummer Gardens, c. 1945
Below: *The Front Entrance* of the original Cummer Home, c. 1945

Agnolo Gaddi, Italian, c. 1350–1396
Madonna of Humility with Angels, mid 1390s
Tempera on panel, $34^1/_2$ x $20^3/_4$
Bequest of Ninah M. H. Cummer

C 130.1

Agnolo Gaddi was heir to the great Florentine painting tradition of Giotto (1266–1337), the acknowledged father of the Italian Renaissance. Gaddi inherited his father's workshop, which he directed very successfully until the end of the fourteenth century. The Cummer panel is rare because it is one of the very few small works completed entirely by Gaddi. His skill is demonstrated in the acute attention to detail, especially in the elaborate tooling and punching of the gold leaf found in the background and halos. Many of these specific punch marks can be seen in Gaddi's other works.

The Madonna is shown suckling the Christ Child while seated on the floor with her head bowed. This humble portrayal of the Madonna became prevalent in fourteenth-century Italian painting and was a result of the humanization of the Virgin Mary as a mother. Two hovering angels hold a crown over her head revealing that the Madonna is also the Queen of Heaven. To emphasize this royal reference, she is clothed in a beautiful blue mantle that is lined in green and trimmed in gold. The robe underneath is decorated with an intricate gold pattern. The patterning is continued in the cloth of honor that is held aloft by two red-clad, red-winged heavenly angels.

ave maria grazia plena

Battista da Vicenza, Italian, c. 1350–1438
St. Bartholomew and *Unidentified Apostle Saint,*
c. 1404–08
Tempera on panel, 7¹/₂ x 5¹/₂
Bequest of Ninah M. H. Cummer

C 139.1 and C 139.2

These gold ground saint panels probably comprised a fraction of an upper tier of figures in a folding altarpiece known as a polyptych. This would explain the shape of the wood panel on which the figures are painted. Traditionally, the saints in the upper tier are shown full length. In these paintings, however, the panels may have been cut down to half-length.

St. Bartholomew, one of the Apostles, was flayed alive during a missionary journey in Armenia. Here he is depicted with a knife and scroll, the symbols of his martyrdom. The other saint lacks any symbolic attribute and may be one of the other Apostles. Both saints are clothed in brilliant robes. St. Bartholomew wears an additional white robe decorated with a gold, star-like pattern.

Most of what is known of Battista da Vicenza comes from two sources: his frescoes in the Church of San Giorgio near Velo d'Astico in northern Italy and his works in the Vicenza Museum, all of which are dated in the first decade of the fifteenth century.
Stylistic comparisons place these two small panels firmly in his oeuvre.

Albrecht Dürer, German, 1471–1528
The Circumcision, 1511
Woodcut on paper, 11⅝ x 8⅛
Cornelia Morse Carithers Memorial Print Collection

AP 1991.3.6

Initially trained as a goldsmith by his father, Albrecht Dürer apprenticed with a designer of woodcuts for book illustrations. He complemented his artistic training with a thorough reading of the major classic authors. He married in 1494 and left Germany for Venice, possibly to escape the plague then raging in Nuremberg, but more probably to study Italian art to which he was particularly attracted. Two years later, he returned to Nuremberg to set up shop, but went again to Venice in 1504 following a renewed outbreak of the plague. He was a key figure in the development of the Northern European Renaissance.

The ritual of the Christ Child's circumcision is described in the apocryphal book the *Life of the Virgin*. In this image, the Virgin Mary is standing in the lower right corner. A crowd of parishioners has gathered around the high priest who performs the rite. The scene takes place in front of an arched portal, representing the transition from one stage of life to the next.

Dürer issued five print cycles in book form, beginning with *The Apocalypse* in 1498. Four of these splendid volumes of woodcuts appeared before the close of 1511. Some of the woodcuts were accompanied by Latin poems. Seventeen of the twenty woodcuts Dürer created to illustrate the *Life of the Virgin* were finished before he went to Venice in 1504.

Lucas Cranach the Elder, German, 1472–1553
St. Christopher and the Christ Child, c. 1518
Oil on panel, $22^3/_4$ x $15^1/_4$
Bequest of Ninah M. H. Cummer

C 203.1

Lucas the Elder was the foremost member of a family of
artists by the name of Cranach working in Saxony in the
sixteenth century. In 1505 he settled in Wittenberg,
where he became court artist to the Electors of Saxony.
There he established a highly productive workshop that
developed a distinct manner of painting that defined the
art of Saxony for the rest of the sixteenth century.

This painting depicts the legend of St. Christopher,
which records a Canaanite of huge stature named Offero
who wanted to serve the most powerful person in the
land. His first master, a king, failed him by fleeing in fear
of Satan. The giant Offero left this king to serve Satan,
whom he also deserted after noticing the devil trembling
in fear before a cross. During his wanderings in search
of the all-powerful Christ, the giant came upon a hermit
who directed him to ferry poor and weak people across
a swollen stream. One night Offero carried a small child
who grew heavier and heavier with each step. With the
aid of a large branch the two reached the opposite shore
where the giant said that he felt he had just carried the
weight of the world. The Child answered that Offero
had, indeed, carried that weight as well as the weight of
the Creator of the world. Offero was later given the
name Christopher, Greek for "Christ-bearer."

Master of the Stötteritz Altar,
German, active late 15th century
Mother of Sorrows, c. 1480
Oil on panel, 8³/₄ x 6¹/₂
Gift of Mrs. Clifford G. Schultz in memory of
Mr. Clifford G. Schultz

AG 1984.1.1

This painting is one of only six known works attributed
to the anonymous artist, whose identity comes from his
association with the Stötteritz Altarpiece, a triptych
located in the church at Leipzig-Stötteritz in Germany.
His work, including this *Mother of Sorrows*, exemplifies
the heightened realism and emotional drama that
characterized Northern Renaissance painting.

With painstaking acuity the artist has articulated the
expressive details of the Madonna's features, costume,
and gesture. Her sorrow is explicitly revealed in her red
swollen eyes and the tears that fall upon her cheeks.
The Madonna extends her left hand to the viewer in a
gesture of intercession, welcoming the prayers of the
faithful. This panel was the left half of a portable hinged
diptych designed for personal devotion. Traditionally, the
subject of the grieving Madonna was paired with an
image of Christ as the *Man of Sorrows*. Mary's gesture of
grasping her mantle can be interpreted as a prelude to
wiping the brow of the suffering Christ in the missing
panel. The window ledge in the foreground enhances
the sense of three-dimensional space, an artistic
technique perfected during the Renaissance, whereas
the flat, gilded background harkens back to more
archaic medieval traditions.

Nicklaus Weckmann the Elder,
German, active 1481–1526
Madonna and Child, c. 1490–1500
Limewood, 47½
Museum purchase with Council funds

AP 1979.2.1

Nicklaus Weckmann the Elder was the leading sculptor
in Ulm, Germany, during the first quarter of the sixteenth
century. He was granted citizenship to the city in 1481,
and was listed in the register of citizens from 1510 to
1526 as "Nicklaus Weckmann, sculptor, the elder."
His workshop produced numerous sculptural programs
for churches throughout southwestern Germany.

This *Madonna and Child* was originally part of a large
winged retable, or altarpiece. With their clear represen-
tations of Biblical narratives, carved altarpieces served
as "the Bibles of the illiterate." Weckmann's naturalistic
Madonna gently cradles an animated Christ child who
holds a pomegranate, a Christian symbol of fertility and
eternity. Many of the altarpiece carvings from this period
were painted, but some artists preferred the beauty of
natural wood. Without the assistance of paint to render
minute detail and realistic texture, their carvings
required greater skill. The masterly execution of
Weckmann's work is evident in the details of Mary's
cascading hair, the folds of her robe, and her tender
expression. Limewood was an ideal material for carving
because of its strong intricate structure, light weight,
and warm ochre color. Limewood trees were also
believed to be holy and were sometimes hung with
inscribed plaques to scare away the plague.

Gerolamo Giovenone, Italian, c. 1490–1555
Christ among the Doctors, 1513
Tempera on panel, 69¼ x 36½
Signed and dated lower left:
HIERONIMI IVVE/NONIS OPIFICE/–1513–
Museum purchase

AP 1981.1.1

Gerolamo Giovenone was born in the northern Italian
region of the Piedmont, which at the time was ruled by
the Dukes of Savoy as part of the Habsburg Empire.
High foreheads, oval-like faces, and finely drawn
mouths, all rendered in strong colors, characterize the
artist's Franco-Flemish style. Giovenone's great attention
to detail in the hair, beards, and intricate robes of the
male figures in the painting are reminiscent of Flemish
art of the preceding century. The Cummer painting is
one of only four works signed and dated by the artist.
It is noteworthy that Giovenone signed the painting as
"goldsmith" (*aurifex* in Latin, *orefice* in Italian) rather
than "painter" (*pictor*, or *pittore*). In written contracts
between artist and patron, much importance was given
to the quality of particular materials, such as
pigments and gold.

This painting depicts an incident from the Bible.
When Jesus was twelve, Joseph and Mary took him to
Jerusalem to celebrate Passover. He wandered off to the
temple, where they found him three days later "sitting
among the teachers, listening to them and asking them
questions; and all who heard him were amazed at his
understanding and his answers" (Luke 2: 46–47).

Pier Francesco de Jacopo Foschi,
Italian, 1502–1567
Bartolomeo Compagni, 1549
Oil on panel, 40½ x 32½
Inscribed and dated right: *1549 ATATE 46*
Museum purchase with Council funds

AP 1984.3.1

Pier Francesco de Jacopo Foschi was active in Florence and received several important commissions, including the creation of paintings for Michelangelo's (1475–1564) funeral. The artist also collaborated on the decorations for the Medici family's Villa of Careggi and was among the select group of artists responsible for planning the Florentine Accademia del Disegno in 1563. Approximately twenty-five portraits are attributed to Foschi, the majority of which show unknown sitters, usually members of the clergy. He favored formal poses, reserved expressions, and direct gazes in his portraiture.

This portrait of Bartolomeo Compagni (1503–1562) is one of two works by Foschi in which the name of the sitter is revealed through inscription. Compagni's name appears on the letter in the foreground and both the date and his age are inscribed on the pilaster at the upper right. Compagni was an exceptionally wealthy Florentine cloth merchant who lived in London from 1535 until his death. Through fair business practices and a series of generous loans, Compagni gained the confidence of Tudor monarchs and was trusted with secret diplomatic missions on behalf of Henry VIII (1491–1547). The still life on the desk and ledge includes an early drum timepiece with a watch key and a signet ring and wax used to personalize and seal important missives. The seal of St. George, patron saint of England, is a reference to Compagni's work in that country.

Giorgio Vasari, Italian, 1511–1574
The Holy Family with the Infant, St. John the Baptist,
c. 1540
Oil on panel, 42¾ x 32⅛
Museum purchase with Council funds

AP 1989.3.1

This fine painting demonstrates Giorgio Vasari's close affiliation with the Mannerist style of painting. Intense, bright colors, an asymmetrical composition, and exaggerations in scale create a dynamic image. The Virgin Mary and St. Joseph are shown as caring parents of the Christ Child, who holds a goldfinch in his left hand. The tiny bird, fond of eating thistles and thorny plants and commonly interpreted as a reference to Christ's crown of thorns, foreshadows his Crucifixion. The inscription on the banderole, *Agnus Dei*, or lamb of God, also suggests his future sacrifice. St. John the Baptist is shown as a young child, already clad in the animal furs that foretell his preaching in the inhospitable wilderness.

The reputation and fame of Vasari is based in large part on his authorship of the *Lives of the Most Eminent Painters, Sculptors, and Architects* (Florence, 1568), an indispensable history of Italian artists. This highly readable book, full of astute observations and amusing anecdotes, laid the foundation for a humanist-inspired art history. As an artist, architect, and writer, Vasari was closely associated with the court of the Medici family in Florence, where he was sent as a young boy of thirteen to receive training in art, geometry, and Latin. Vasari's artistic activities and success contributed immensely to a heightened appreciation of the social status of the Renaissance artist.

Workshop of Guido Durantino,
Italian, active 1520–1576
Maiolica Plate, c. 1540
Ceramic, 17³/₄
Museum purchase with membership contributions

AP 1968.1.1

The workshop overseen by Guido Durantino and his son, Orazio Fontana, dominated *maiolica* production in Urbino throughout the sixteenth century. Originally deriving its name from the metallic lusterware imported through the Spanish island of Majorca, the pottery style referred to as *maiolica* reached a peak of artistic and economic value during the Italian Renaissance. Newly developed glazes, kiln designs, inventive decorative schemes, and well-trained craftsmen distinguished Italian production from more conservative Spanish works.

Often the decorations on *maiolica* are derived from other sources. This plate design is based on an etching by the Veronese artist Torbido del Moro, after a c.1530 wood-cut. The woodcut reproduced details from a painting by the Venetian artist Titian (c. 1485–1576). The *maiolica* painter expertly reconceived the original rectangular design to fit the circular format of the plate. Maintained in the translation from etching to pottery is the sweep of space that is punctuated by the central grouping of men milking and feeding their cattle, a goat ascending the steep embankment, and herdsmen resting beneath a canopy of trees. Their graceful branches lead the viewer to the distant walled village and ship at anchor.

Pieter Aertsen, Dutch, 1507/08–1575
The Parable of the Marriage Feast, 1550–1554
Oil on panel, 48½ x 66½
Museum purchase with Council funds

AP 1965.12.1

Pieter Aertsen was trained in Amsterdam, but worked for much of his career in Antwerp, where he enrolled in the Guild of St. Luke as a master painter. He was particularly known for his important religious paintings and monumental genre scenes. This is one of his most important large religious works because it survived the *Beeldenstorm* of 1566, a rebellious event in the Netherlands during which religious paintings and sculptures were destroyed. Later in life, Aertsen returned to his native Amsterdam and remained there until his death.

The large size of this work permits the artist to depict a continuous narrative in one painting. The subject of this very involved picture comes from the Bible. In Matthew 22 verses 1-14, Jesus describes how a king invited his subjects to celebrate the marriage of his son. When no one came to the marriage feast, the king commanded his servants to go out and collect people both "good and bad" to attend the event. As the king observed his guests, he noticed one who did not wear the appropriate attire for the celebration. Because of this infraction, the king had the man bound and cast into darkness. The parable of the marriage feast ends with the words "many are called, but few are chosen."

One of the most striking aspects of this scene is the combination of ancient ruins with contemporary sixteenth-century architectural elements from Rome. These kinds of buildings were known through the many drawings and prints done by other northern artists traveling to Rome.

Pieter Bruegel, Flemish, c. 1525/30–1569
Envy (Invidia), from the *Series of the Seven
Deadly Sins,* 1558
Engraving on paper, 8³/₄ x 11¹/₂
Museum purchase with contribution given in memory of
Mr. & Mrs. Joseph Morrel Dodge

AP 1971.2.1

The bizarre imagery of Pieter Bruegel's paintings and
prints is deeply rooted in the artist's humanist learning
and personal knowledge of Flemish popular culture and
language. A resentful woman in the center of the print
who is seen "eating her heart out" personifies Envy, one
of the Seven Deadly Sins. Behind the woman is a hollow
tree, wherein lurks a monster. Peacock feathers are the
tree's only growth. The many references to shoes in this
engraving find their origins in a number of Flemish
proverbs. These sayings allude to living beyond one's
financial means, excessive display of material wealth,
insatiable self-love, and Pride, the mother of Envy.

Pieter Bruegel was a painter, humanist, draftsman, and
printmaker. After joining the Guild of St. Luke in
Antwerp, he traveled to Italy and went as far south as
Naples. Unlike other artists of his time, he even visited
Messina and Palermo on the island of Sicily. His paint-
ings were much sought after by royal patrons in Madrid,
Brussels, and Prague.

Often his drawings served as publishing material for
other printmakers. In this instance, the invention and
drawing of the *Seven Deadly Sins* are Bruegel's, whereas
the engravings were made by Pieter van der Heyden
(active c. 1550–c. 1580) and published by Hieronymous
Cock (1507–1570), a painter turned engraver and
publisher who owned the printing house "In the Four
Winds." This division of labor is indicated on the print,
showing the names of the three artists and business
partners, followed by abbreviations in Latin detailing
their part in this collaborative venture.

· INVIDIA ·

INVIDIA HORRENDVM MONSTRVM, SÆVISSIMA PESTIS ·
Een onsterffelijcke doot es nijt / en vreede peste Een beest die haer seluen eet / met valschen moleste

Theodor de Bry, Flemish, 1528–1598
Meeting between René de Laudonnière and the Timucuan Chief Athore,
from: *Grands Voyages,* vol. 2, plate VIII, 1591
Engraving, 12 $\frac{7}{8}$ x 9 $\frac{3}{8}$
Gift of Ms. Constance I. & Mr. Ralph H. Wark

AG 1973.19.1

This print shows one of the earliest events in recorded Florida history, which took place in what is now known as Jacksonville. In 1564, a French Huguenot expedition under the leadership of René de Laudonnière landed near the mouth of the St. Johns River. Chief Athore of the Timucuan indigenous group welcomed the French and led them to see "a remarkable thing." As an early travel account relates, "Athore conducted them to a hillock where an earlier French expedition led by Jean Ribault had erected a stone column engraved with the arms of the king of France. On approaching the column the French saw the Indians worshipping the stone as an idol." The same travel account mentions that Athore, "was a handsome man, wise, honorable and strong, more than half a foot taller than even the tallest of our men." The site of this encounter has been identified as Fort Caroline, just south of Amelia Island.

The print was executed and published by Theodor de Bry, member of an influential Flemish family. De Bry faithfully followed a drawing prepared by Jacques Le Moyne de Morgues, an artist who accompanied the Laudonnière expedition. His instructions were "to map the sea coast, and harbors... and portray the dwellings of the natives and anything else in the land worthy of observation." All of Le Moyne's drawings have since been lost, except the one that served as a model for this engraving. It is noteworthy that the original Le Moyne drawing and subsequent de Bry engravings are the only known visual documentation of the customs and appearance of the now extinct Timucua.

Columnam à Præfecto prima navigatione locatam VIII. venerantur Floridenses.

V M. Galli in Floridam provinciam, secunda navigatione instituta duce Laudonniero, appulis-
sent, ipse comitibus quinque & viginti pyxidarijs in continentem descendit, salute ab Indis ac
cepta (nam catervatim ad eos conspiciendos advenerant) Rex Athoré quatuor aut quinq; mi
liaribus à maris littore habitans etiam venit, & muneribus datis & acceptis, omnique humani
tatis genere exhibito, indicavit se singulare quidpiam ipsis demonstrare velle, propterea orare ut
una proficiscerentur: adsentiuntur, quia tamen magno subditorum numero cinctum videbant, cautè & circumspe-
ctè cum eo profecti sunt. Ille verò eos in insulam deduxit, in qua Ribaldus super tumulo quodam saxeum limitem
insignibus Regis Galliæ insculptum posuerat. Proximi facti, animadverterunt Indos hoc saxum non secus atque
idolum colere: nam ipse Rex eo salutato, & exhibito qualem à suis subditis accipere solet honore, osculo fixit, quem
imitati sunt ipsius subditi, ut idem faceremus adhortati. Ante saxum jacebant varia donaria fructibus ejus regio-
nis & radicibus edulibus, vel ad medicum usum utilibus constantia, vasaque plena odoratis oleis, arcus & sagittæ:
cinctum etiam erat, ab imo ad summum, florum omnis generis corollis, & arborum apud ipsos selectissimarum ra-
mis. Perspecto miserorum horum barbarorum ritu, ad suos redierunt observaturi commodissimum ad propugnacu-
lum extruendum locum. Est verò hic Rex Athoré formosus admodum, prudens, honestus, robustus & proceræ admodum staturæ, nostrorum hominu maximos sesquipeda superans, modesta quadam gravitate præditus, ut in eo ma-
jestas spectabilis reluceat. Cum matre matrimonium contraxit, & ex ea plures liberos utriusq; sexus suscepit, quos
percusso fœmore nobis ostendit: postquam verò ipsi desponsata fuit, parens ejus Satuioua illam amplius non attigit

Anonymous Elizabethan
Portrait of a Lady, 1592
Oil on panel, 26 x 18¼
Dated upper left: *ANNo 1592*
Bequest of Ninah M. H. Cummer

C 153.1

The identity of this richly attired sitter is unknown, but the attention the anonymous artist paid to her costume, especially to the delicate and fashionable lace collar, indicates her high social status. Typical of English portraits created during the prosperous reign of Elizabeth I, from 1558 to 1603, the painting features a flattened sense of space and minimal modeling of the figure. This conscious rejection of naturalism reflects the strict Protestant teachings of the time, which frowned upon both the creation of religious imagery and attempts to imitate life in art.

The Latin inscription to the right of the sitter alludes to her Protestant beliefs and translates, "The image which you perceive is neither God nor a human. But what the image signifies is both God and human." This motto was designed to remind the viewer that a painted image could not replace an actual human being, or in religious art, the deity. The inclusion of a small Bible or Book of Psalms serves as a reminder that Protestants believed in the primacy of the Bible in all matters concerning religious teachings and opposed the Catholic reliance on images as devotional aids.

Hendrick Goltzius, Dutch, 1558–1617 and
Jacob Matham, Dutch, 1571–1631
The Fates, c. 1590
Engraving on paper, 10¼ x 8⅛
Cornelia Morse Carithers Memorial Print Collection

AP 1990.7.1

Hendrick Goltzius was an important draftsman, print–
maker, and painter in the northern Netherlands at a
time when the Seven United Provinces were experi-
encing political upheaval. He was particularly famed
for the technical virtuosity of his prints and the way his
burin lines swelled and thinned to create lights and
darks and tones and volumes in his figures. After a
long career as a pre-eminent engraver, Goltzius gave
up printmaking in 1600 to take up the palette and
brush and become a painter.

Jacob Matham was Goltzius's stepson and apprentice
and his primary charge was to engrave many of the
master's drawings. He imitated Goltzius's manner and
worked more closely with him than any other in his
stepfather's circle of engravers. This print comes from
a series of mythological subjects and depicts the Three
Fates spinning the thread of life and measuring and
cutting off an allotted amount. Clotho is standing and
holding the distaff, Lachesis is holding the spindle, while
Atropos, the most terrible of the three, snips the thread
with her shears. In classical mythology, the Fates were
believed to determine a person's destiny.

Id. Inuent.

Workshop of Abraham Bloemaert,
Dutch, 1566–1651
The Baptism of Christ, c. 1593
Oil on panel, 54¹/₂ x 77
Museum purchase

AP 1961.1.1

The authorship of this *Baptism* has been the source of much scholarly debate. It is clearly derived from a painting that was signed by Abraham Bloemaert and dated in 1592. The signed work depicted Apollo and Daphne and was lost in World War II. In comparing the Cummer painting with photographs of the work, small compositional changes can be seen in the background and in some of the details of the foreground. Some scholars believe that the Cummer painting is a sixteenth-century copy of a lost *Baptism* because of its seemingly lesser quality. The question of quality, however, may stem from the fact that the Cummer painting has suffered damage and has been over-cleaned. If this painting is a studio copy done in the presence of the original, it is an important record of a substantial, lost work.

A painter, draftsman, writer, and teacher, Abraham Bloemaert was one of the principal painters in Utrecht in the first half of the seventeenth century. Utrecht was an important artistic center with a taste for Catholic subjects. The city was ideal for Bloemaert and the many students he taught over the years. During his long career, Bloemaert was highly regarded for his religious and mythological works and his approximately 1500 drawings.

17

Jacob de Gheyn II, Flemish, 1565–1629
Christ Crowned with Thorns, c.1600
Watercolor and gouache on vellum, 6¹/₂ x 4³/₄
Museum purchase

AP 1967.18.2

Jacob de Gheyn II was an accomplished draftsman, engraver, and painter who was first trained by his father and then by the renowned engraver Hendrick Goltzius (1558–1617), an artist whose work is represented in the Cummer collection. De Gheyn lived and worked in the Dutch cities of Haarlem, Leiden, and The Hague where he remained until his death. While in The Hague, de Gheyn worked for Prince Maurice of Orange-Nassau (1567–1625) and was an esteemed member of the Guild of St. Luke.

Around 1600, de Gheyn began to turn away from the influence of Goltzius. The lines in his prints and drawings became more fluid and he developed a more naturalistic style. It was also at this time that de Gheyn, using the technique of a miniaturist, began a series of watercolor and gouache drawings on vellum, or calfskin. He used very small brushes to create a delicate stippling that modeled his figures in brilliant colors. One of de Gheyn's trademark characteristics was to highlight these small works with touches of gold. All of these tendencies are evident in this work, especially the gold highlights found in the rays emanating from the head of Christ as he is crowned with thorns.

Cornelis van der Voort, Flemish, c. 1576–1624
Portrait of a Gentleman, 1617
Oil on canvas, 39 x 38½
Inscribed and dated upper right:
AETs SVE 63 Ao 1617
Morton R. Hirschberg Memorial Fund

AP 1988.2.2

A sixty-three year old man looks at the viewer, his eyes betraying a slight apprehension at being portrayed in these fancy clothes. His identity is lost, as is that of his wife, his junior by eighteen years, whose age is indicated in Latin on the painting. Both portraits were painted by the Flemish artist Cornelis van der Voort, who fled his native Antwerp in the southern Netherlands after the city fell to the Spanish in 1585 and emigrated to the recently formed Dutch Republic. Van der Voort settled in Amsterdam and became one of the city's leading portraitists. He was elected head of the Guild of St. Luke, which united the professional painters in that city.

The custom of double portraiture invariably called for the man to be on the left, turned toward the woman. In this position, he "introduces" her to the world. The serious demeanor of this well-dressed and affluent couple reflects the social and ethical values of the young Dutch Protestant Republic. Their sober, yet elegant black clothes evoke "the embarrassment of riches" many Dutch burghers experienced in a time of economic expansion, political successes, and strong Calvinist religious persuasions.

Cornelis van der Voort, Flemish, c. 1576–1624
Portrait of a Lady, 1617
Oil on canvas, 39 x 38½
Inscribed and dated upper left:
AETs SVAE 45 Ao 1617
Morton R. Hirschberg Memorial Fund

AP 1988.2.1

Peter Paul Rubens, Flemish, 1577–1640
The Lamentation of Christ, c. 1605
Oil on copper, 11 x 9¹/₂
Bequest of Ninah M. H. Cummer

C 131.1

Peter Paul Rubens, the son of a prominent Flemish family, was initially destined to become a courtier. He persuaded his mother to let him devote himself to painting. He left for Italy in 1600 and remained there for eight years until his mother's illness forced him to return to Antwerp. Rubens's study of ancient art and Italian painting profoundly influenced his artistic style. He established a studio, received significant commissions, and taught many pupils. After the death of his first wife in 1626, Rubens entered the diplomatic service and made several trips to England and Spain. He was a man of such wide-ranging intellectual learning and abilities that some of his contemporaries considered his artistic gifts to be among the least of his talents. He was fluent in Latin, French, German, Italian, Dutch, and Spanish. Rubens was also a gifted diplomat and was widely read in classical literature, Christian thought, and contemporary affairs.

This painting depicts the scene after Christ's descent from the cross and before his entombment. The Virgin Mary leans over the body of Christ while Mary Magdalene kneels at his feet. Joseph of Arimathea, Nicodemus, and lamenting women complete the circle of mourners. The back of the painting bears the seal of the noble Colonna family of Rome. The work is listed in the 1783 inventory of art treasures in the Colonna palace outside Rome. From 1605 to 1606, Rubens's brother Philip was secretary and librarian to Cardinal Ascanio Colonna (1559–1608), and it is likely that the Cardinal commissioned this picture. It was later given to the painter Giuseppe Cades (1750–1799), whose signed declaration of ownership remains on the back.

Palma Giovane (Jacopo Negretti),
Italian, 1544–1628
Rest on the Return from Egypt, 1625
Ink and wash on paper, 8¼ x 11¾
Signed and dated lower left: *Palma 1625*
Inscribed upper center: *Carlo*
Gift of Joseph Jeffers Dodge

AG 1996.2.72

This drawing depicts Jesus as a young boy resting with Mary and Joseph on their journey from Egypt to Israel. The subject of this drawing should not be confused with the more popular depiction of the Holy Family at rest on their flight into Egypt to escape from Herod's search for the infant Jesus (Matt. 2:13–15). Herod had decreed that all children in Bethlehem under the age of two be killed in what was later called the Massacre of the Innocents. The Holy Family fled to Egypt where they remained until the death of Herod. When they were called to return to Israel, they left Egypt to settle in Nazareth (Matt. 2:19–23). On their return, they met John the Baptist who was preaching in the wilderness where John baptized Jesus.

Palma heralded from a leading family of Italian painters and draftsmen and was considered the foremost painter in Venice in the early seventeenth century. He was a prolific artist and produced more than six hundred paintings and many preparatory drawings. Drawings have always being popular and sought after by collectors, not only for their spontaneity and immediacy of execution, but also for the way they demonstrate the artist's creative processes. This drawing is stamped on the lower right with what appear to be an interlocking "R" and "U," indicating that it came from an established collection, although the collection remains unidentified. Collectors stamps were very popular in the eighteenth and nineteenth centuries and are useful today in determining the provenance, or collecting history, of a work of art.

Frans Snyders, Flemish, 1579–1657
Still Life with Fruit and Flowers, c. 1630
Oil on panel, 31 x 45³/₄
Signed lower right: *F. Snyders fecit*
Morton R. Hirschberg Memorial Fund

AP 1984.1.1

An opulent display of fruit, flowers, and precious objects
takes center stage in this painting by the Flemish artist
Frans Snyders. He is considered one of the greatest
masters of still life painting, a category of art that
specializes in the skillful rendering of quietly appealing
scenes of inanimate objects to produce a decorative and
rhythmical composition. Snyders's painting can be interpreted as an allegory of nature. The freshly cut flowers
may refer to the brevity and passing nature of life; the
tiny knight perched atop the golden chalice on the left is
probably a reference to "the Christian soldier"; and the
grapes are often seen as a symbol of the wine used in
the Eucharist, and hence of Christ's blood.

Snyders's father was the keeper of a well-known
Antwerp inn favored by artists. Following a thorough
apprenticeship, Snyders was made a junior member of
the Antwerp painters' guild at the age of twenty-three
and became a regular member seventeen years later.
In 1608 he went to Italy, the obligatory tour of duty of
any young artist, and returned to Antwerp after fifteen
months. Upon his death, Snyders was a respected
and distinguished painter who left a valuable estate,
including an important art collection.

23

Theodoor Rombouts, Flemish, 1597–1637
The Concert (A Musical Party), c. 1620
Oil on canvas, 44¹/₂ x 69
Museum purchase with funds provided by
Eunice Pitt Odom Semmes

AP 1970.10.1

Theodoor Rombouts studied in Italy from 1616 to 1625,
following an apprenticeship in the vibrant and commer-
cial city of Antwerp in the early seventeenth century.
He was in Rome in 1620 and may have worked for the
Medici in Florence until 1625, when he returned to
Antwerp. Rombouts became a master at the Guild of St.
Luke and embarked on a distinguished career producing
mainly secular works for private patrons.

The Concert depicts a group of costumed musicians
playing various instruments around a table covered with
a Persian tapestry rug. Music parties of this type were
typical subjects for Flemish artists during the seventeenth
century. This painting shows the play of deep shadows
and bright highlights that reflect the strong influence of
the Italian Baroque artist Caravaggio (1571–1610), whose
paintings Rombouts studied during his years in Rome.
Caravaggio's works were characterized by dramatic
figures depicted with unflinching realism.

This music party is a celebration of the five senses.
Rombouts indicates the various senses by selectively
illuminating an ear, nose, hand, and eyes, but omits the
sense of taste. This fifth sense may be represented by the
foremost figure who looks out, inviting the viewer to
complete the circle of senses and welcoming the patron of
"good taste" who commissioned Rombouts's paintings.

24

Workshop of Gian Lorenzo Bernini,
Italian, 1598–1680
Armand Jean du Plessis, Cardinal de Richelieu,
c. 1641
Marble, 26
Gift of Mr. & Mrs. Edward W. Lane, Jr.

AG 1970.7.1

Cardinal de Richelieu (1585–1642) was a man of
respectable but humble origins who became the chief
minister of King Louis XIII (1601–1643) in 1624 and,
eventually, the virtual ruler of France. Bernini completed
a marble portrait bust of the Cardinal in 1640. The pre-
eminent sculptor and architect of his day, Bernini's work
is characterized by the dramatic play of light and dark
seen in the deep carving of this piece. The solemn,
piercing gaze of the Cardinal and the slipped button on
his lapel silently convey the dynamic tension for which
the artist was known.

This sculpture is one of several nearly identical marble
portrait busts of Richelieu credited to Bernini's workshop
or assistants. Similarities between the drill marks and
details found on this bust and the original, at the Musée
du Louvre in Paris, suggest that this marble was created
in Bernini's studio in the presence of the original.
Bernini executed the original bust in Rome while
Cardinal Richelieu was in France. Access to a triple
portrait of the cardinal by Philippe de Champaigne
(1602–1674), showing Richelieu from three angles,
made it possible for Bernini to carve a close likeness.
The number of seventeenth-century copies of this work
attests to the popularity of the original at a time when
studio assistants were producing sought-after replicas
under the supervision of their master.

Gioacchino Assereto, Italian, 1600–1649
The Lamentation, c. 1640
Oil on canvas, 50 x 62
Museum purchase with Council funds

AP 1988.1.1

This dramatic tableau was meant to fulfill the Counter-Reformation Catholic Church's doctrine that art was to "sting the heart," making the viewer see and feel every aspect of the life and death of Christ. Here, the greatly foreshortened pallid body of Christ forms a diagonal that draws the viewer into the midst of the emotional scene, completing the circle of mourners. The play of dark shadows and bright highlights over the surface of the painting theatrically intensifies the sorrow-filled moment. Gioacchino Assereto's *Lamentation* depicts Christ descended from the Cross and laid upon a cloth on the ground. Mourning him are the Virgin Mary who is near his head, Mary Magdalene who kisses his hand in a penitent gesture, and St. John the Evangelist who holds the crown of thorns.

Assereto worked in Genoa, Italy and specialized in painting religious subjects. He visited Rome in 1639 where he experienced firsthand the burgeoning interest in realism. This work is one of the very few paintings by Assereto found outside of Italy. Most of his paintings are still in the churches and *palazzi* for which they were originally commissioned.

Claude Lorrain (Claude Gellée),
French, 1600–1682
Minerva Visiting the Muses on Mount Parnassus, 1680
Oil on canvas, 57 x 76
Signed and dated bottom right:
Clauvdio IV Roma 1680
Bequest of Ninah M. H. Cummer

C 110.1

Claude Lorrain, named after the region in northeastern France where he was born, went to Italy at the age of thirteen and remained there until his death, making only one trip to his native region in 1625. He acquired enormous fame as a classical landscape artist, creating ideal images of nature more beautiful and better ordered than nature itself. Carefully integrated elements of ancient architecture and culture in Claude's paintings reflect courtly values of high finish and decorum. As a result, his most important clients were members of the European nobility and high clergy.

In this scene Minerva, the Roman goddess of wisdom, visits Mount Parnassus in Greece. The mountain is located in the vicinity of Delphi and was known for its springs, one of which was called Hippocrene. This spring was venerated as a source of inspiration and was consecrated to Apollo and the nine Muses, the goddesses

of the arts and sciences. As told by Ovid in his *Metamorphoses,* Minerva said to Urania, the Muse who welcomed her, "I have heard that you now have a new and wondrous fount. It burst out from the ground beneath the winged horse Pegasus' hard hoof. I've come to see this marvel.... And Minerva looked at length at where the waters had sprung up. And her eyes took in the ancient forests, the inmost groves, the grottoes, and the flowers."

Claude included a sketch of this painting, no. 195, in his *Liber veritatis* (*Book of Truth*), a unique book of drawings created by the artist to record his paintings. Claude probably executed this painting, a remarkable example of his mature style, for Prince don Lorenzo Onofrio Colonna (1637–1689). Coincidentally, a member of the same noble family owned the *Lamentation* by Rubens, also on display in the Cummer.

27

Paulus Bor, Dutch, 1601–1669
Allegory of Avarice
Oil on canvas, 48 x 39 3/8
Bequest of Ninah M. H. Cummer

C 128.1

The old, miserly looking woman embodies the deadly sin of greed. She sits on a low stool amidst moneybags and pots of coins. Her homely spindle is discarded on the floor and the fire and lamp are extinguished. A snarling dog lies on an empty moneybag. The legal document hanging over the parapet suggests the hold the woman has over her debtors. A string of onions hangs on the wall—often a reference to old women as procurers of illicit love.

In 1793, this painting entitled *Avarice* was illustrated in a French book of engravings and ascribed to Rembrandt. Experts do not always agree on the authorship of a particular painting, and *Allegory of Avarice* is a good example. Following Rembrandt, a number of Dutch artists, most persuasively Paulus Bor, have been mentioned in association with this painting.

Paulus Bor, a member of a wealthy and prominent Catholic family in Amersfoort near Utrecht, studied in Italy. He was a founding member of the *Schildersbent*, an informal association of Dutch artists and bohemians living in Rome, and was known to his companions as "Orlando." Returning to his native city after three years in Italy, Bor established a successful studio where he executed, among other commissions, paintings for the palace of Prince Frederick Henry of Orange-Nassau (1584–1647) at Honselaarsdijk.

28

Sassoferrato (Giovanni Battista Salvi),
Italian, 1609–1685
Praying Madonna, c. 1660
Oil on canvas, 17³/₄ x 14
Museum purchase with membership contributions

AP 1968.17.1

Sassoferrato, whose name means "iron stone," was named after the town in which he was born and was originally trained by his father before continuing his studies in Rome. For the first half of his career, Sassoferrato worked on major church fresco projects and on portraits of noble families and members of the clergy.

From 1650 until his death, Sassoferrato worked almost exclusively on images of the Madonna. His paintings were in great demand because of the revitalization of the cult of the Virgin Mary during the Counter-Reformation. It is well documented that he was obliged to paint the image of the Madonna in quantity and to keep a reserve stock to meet the ever-increasing requests of his clientele.

In the New Testament, there are only two references to the Madonna in prayer—at the Annunciation and at the Adoration of the Christ Child. This painting of the Madonna looking down tenderly at the Child as she prays illustrates the latter. Here, Mary is the merciful mother, and in the eyes of the Counter-Reformation Church she depicts the finest attributes of a woman.

29

Reynaud Levieux de Nîmes, French, 1613–1699
Theseus Discovering His Father's Sword, c. 1643
Oil on canvas, 44 $^5/_8$ x 52$^1/_2$
Gift of Eunice Pitt Odom Semmes

AP 1963.5.1

Reynaud Levieux, the son of a Protestant glass painter,
was born and raised in Nîmes in the South of France.
In 1640 Levieux went to Rome and made drawings after
paintings by the Italian Renaissance master Raphael
(1483–1520). These drawings were intended as designs
for tapestries to be woven in France. Levieux returned to
Nîmes four years later, where he remained for the next
twenty-five years, establishing a substantial reputation.
In 1669, Levieux returned to Rome, but continued to
paint for clients and church patrons who lived in the
South of France. Despite his Protestant upbringing,
Levieux spent his last years as a Carthusian monk.

This episode is taken from the legend of the Greek hero
Theseus, famous slayer of the Minotaur on the island of
Crete. Theseus is shown as a young man, moving a large
stone that covers a sword and sandals left by his father
Aegeus following the night of Theseus's conception.
According to a prediction made by the oracle at Delphi,
he who could move the rock and recover these articles
would be recognized by Aegeus as his son. The woman
in the painting's center is Theseus's mother Aethra.

Levieux's art is refined in coloring and execution, and
the features of the actors in his paintings are dignified
and austere, typical aspects of the seventeenth-century
classical Baroque style in France. This painting,
created during Levieux's first Roman sojourn,
demonstrates his exceptional talent as a painter of
ancient architecture, which has been rendered with
erudition and understanding.

30

Sir Peter Lely (Pieter van der Faes),
English, 1618–1680
The Countess of Radnor, Letitia Isabella Smith,
c. 1647
Oil on canvas, 50 x 40
Gift of Dr. & Mrs. Robert P. Coggins

AG 1974.24.1

Dutch by birth, Peter Lely assumed the name of his house *"in de Lelye"* because of the lily carved on the roof gable. As a painter, draftsman, and collector, Lely established himself in London in the mid-seventeenth century and became the leading portrait painter in England. Named a Principal Painter in 1661 by King Charles II (1630–1685), he was naturalized as an English citizen in 1662 and was knighted in 1680.

Lely's sensuous handling of graceful forms and rich fabrics reached its peak by 1650. His artistic maturity can be seen at its best in this portrait of the Countess of Radnor. From the languid, almost dreamy pose of the bejeweled sitter, to the exquisite shimmering satins that enhance her porcelain skin, this portrait is a tour-de-force of visual richness. Lely has used golden highlights throughout the picture to accentuate her youthful beauty. This painting was most likely commissioned by John Robartes, Earl of Radnor, at the time of his engagement or marriage to his second wife Letitia Smith.

31

Pieter Thijs, Flemish, 1624–1677 and **Pieter Boel,**
Flemish, 1622–1674
Huntsman with His Dogs and Game, c. 1650
Oil on canvas, 72 x 103½
Gift of Samuel H. Kress Foundation

AG 1961.9.1

This life-size portrait of an unknown hunter is
considered to be the collaborative work of Pieter Thijs
and Pieter Boel. Both artists were born in Antwerp and
became members of the Guild of St. Luke in 1644 and
1650 respectively. Credited with the image of the hunter
in this painting, Thijs was known for large-scale
religious compositions and elegant portraits. The game
and dogs are attributed to Pieter Boel, a specialist in
animal painting who was an accomplished still life
painter. Boel was active in France after 1668 and served
as *Peintre Ordinaire* to Louis XIV (1638–1715).
While in France, Boel produced tapestry designs for
the Gobelins factory and made studies of animals in
the royal menagerie.

Collaborative efforts between artists were not uncommon
at the time; specialists in areas such as portraiture,
landscape, or still life often worked cooperatively to
accommodate the wishes of a patron. Hunting scenes
became popular artistic subjects in the Netherlands during
the seventeenth century. The sport was a favorite among
the nobility and was also enjoyed by the wealthy
merchant class. Images of hunters with the abundance of
their sport were often commissioned to commemorate
specific events and desired for their decorative value.

32

Jan Steen, Dutch, 1626–1679
The Continence of Scipio, late 1660s
Oil on canvas, 34¹/₂ x 58¹/₂
Signed lower left: *Jan Steen*
Museum purchase with funds from the
Frederick H. Schultz family & the Cummer Council

AP 2000.1.1

The artist Jan Steen was the first of eight children from the marriage of Havick Steen and Elisabeth Capiteyn, both members of established, well-to-do families. Jan Steen attended Latin school and enrolled in the University of Leiden for a brief time. In 1648 he registered in the Guild of St. Luke as a master painter. His reputation is based on his comical depictions of every-day life, particularly scenes of chaotic family settings. These popular images gave rise to the Dutch proverb "a Jan Steen household," meaning an untidy and unruly home. In 1721 his first biographer wrote, "His paintings are like his way of life and his way of life like his paintings," a view that took particular hold in the Romantic imagination of Steen's art and life.

This painting represents the serious side of Steen's artistic oeuvre, although satire and mockery are also present. The Roman general Scipio Africanus Major (237–183 B.C.), after conquering the Spanish town of New Carthage (present-day Cartagena), was presented with precious gifts and honors. Among those spoils was a beautiful young maiden. When Scipio learned that she was engaged to be married, he summoned her fiancé and returned the young woman to him. The bridegroom, the woman's parents, and the onlookers expressed their gratitude for this admirable example of the classical virtue of continence, or self-restraint and discipline. The story, adapted from the Roman and Greek historians Livy and Polybius, is represented with great theatricality and anachronistic details. The artist focuses on the magnanimity and spirit of the gesture at the expense of archaeological and historical precision.

70

33

Carl Andreas Ruthart, German, 1630–1703
David Called From His Flock, c. 1672
Oil on canvas, 38½ x 65
Museum purchase

AP 1962.2.1

The German-born artist Carl Ruthart visited Rome in
1659 and went to Antwerp in 1663, where he became
a member of the Guild of St. Luke and studied Flemish
animal painting. He returned to Italy and worked in
Venice until the 1670s when he went to Rome. Ruthart
was especially known for his dramatic animal scenes
and adeptness at depicting animal anatomy and fur.

The subject of this painting comes from the First Book
of Samuel (16:11-13). The prophet Samuel called for the
sons of Jesse to pass before him because he had been
told by God that a new king of the Israelites was to be
found among them. The prophet asked if all the sons
were present, and upon learning that one son, David,
was keeping the sheep, he sent for him. Upon his
arrival, God said to Samuel of David, "this is he," and
Samuel anointed him as the future king.

This painting was reproduced in an engraving by Pietro
Monaco (1710–c. 1775) in Venice in the eighteenth
century. The inscription on the engraving gives the
authorship of the work to Ruthart and indicates
the painting was in the collection of the noble Manfrotti
family at San Samuele in Venice. This documentation
enables the painting to be seen as a pendant to the
work by Ruthart, *David Called Before the Prophet Samuel,*
in the Musée du Louvre in Paris.

Jacques de Claeuw (Jacques Grief),
Dutch, active 1642–1677
Vanitas, 1677
Oil on canvas, 37 x 49³/₄
Signed at left edge of table: *J D Claeu*
Gift of Eunice Pitt Odom Semmes

AP 1962.3.1

Jacques Grief was born in Dordrecht, a small river town
in northern Holland. Because of a physical deformity,
he was given the nickname of "de Claeuw" meaning
"the claw." The artist, a brother-in-law of the painter Jan
Steen (1626–1679), was known for his still life images.
Popularized as an independent genre by Dutch artists
of the period, still life appealed to the taste of Calvinist
patrons who objected to overtly religious art.

The term *vanitas* (Latin for "emptiness") is applied to still
life images featuring objects that represent the brevity
of life or the emptiness of worldly concerns. De Claeuw's
contemporary public was familiar with such symbolism
and would have recognized the partially covered celestial
globe as an attribute of astronomy. The globe, along with
a copy of the *Amsterdam Waersegger Almanach* (1677),
a soothsayer's almanac, refers to man's inability to
accurately predict the future. The musical instruments,
inkwell, sealing wax, and cards refer to the vanity of
worldly amusements. The hourglass and the smoke
associated with the pipe and candle denote the passage
of time. Flies and flowers are symbolic of decay and the
shortness of life. The image of Venus refers to the
impermanence of physical beauty. A small portrait of the
prominent engraver Pieter de Jode (1604–1674) is a
reference to the immortality an artist attempts to
gain through art.

35

Alexandre de Comans, French, active c. 1650
Rinaldo Carried to Armida's Enchanted Chariot,
c. 1650
After designs by **Simon Vouet,** French, 1590–1649
Wool and silk tapestry, 123 x 172
Monogrammed bottom right: *AC and RVPL*(?)
Gift of Eunice Pitt Odom Semmes

AP 1962.5.1

The coat of arms prominently displayed at the top of this tapestry indicates that it was commissioned by François Petit de Villeneuve and Marie-Anne de Faucault, members of the French aristocracy. The tapestry was woven at the Parisian tapestry works of the Comans family who emigrated from Antwerp in 1601. This tapestry is from a set of five designed after a series of paintings by the French artist Simon Vouet (1590–1649). Both the paintings and the tapestries illustrate scenes from the popular epic poem *Jerusalem Delivered* (1581) by the Italian poet Torquato Tasso (1544–1595).

Set during the first Crusade (1099), *Jerusalem Delivered* was a combination of historical fact and fantasy. The theme "love conquers all" was popular in seventeenth-century art and literature. In this scene, the beautiful sorceress Armida, though originally determined to defeat the crusaders who invaded her homeland, falls in love with her sleeping enemy Rinaldo. With the assistance of her attendants, Armida binds Rinaldo with chains of flowers and prepares to carry him to her fortress in the Fortunate Isles aboard her chariot.

Alessandro Gherardini, Italian, 1655–1723
The Forge of Vulcan, c. 1688
Oil on canvas, 31³/₈ x 40¹/₂
Gifts of Mr. & Mrs. S. Kendrick Guernsey

AG 1972.15.1

Alessandro Gherardini spent most of his career in Florence completing commissions to decorate numerous churches and the interiors of well-known villas and *palazzi.* He traveled extensively and his paintings show the influence of the major artists working in the areas he visited.

The narratives for these two paintings are drawn from various classical authors. As seen in the first painting, Virgil's *Aeneid* records in Book VIII that Venus, the mother of Aeneas, pleaded with her husband Vulcan to create armor to protect her son. *The Forge of Vulcan* illustrates the god of fire and his Cyclops helpers as they create a

breastplate for Aeneas. The second painting depicts the story of the Nereid Amphitrite, as told by both Homer in the *Odyssey* and by Hesiod in the *Theogony*. Though no specific part of the myth is illustrated here, this image of Amphitrite with the sea god Neptune shows her triumphant in love.

Classical gods and goddesses were often used to symbolize the four elements. Here, the forge of Vulcan represents Fire and the scene with Amphitrite and Neptune, Water. Typically, the goddesses Ceres or Cybele would have represented Earth, and Hera, wife of Zeus, would have stood for Air.

Alessandro Gherardini, Italian, 1655–1723
The Triumph of Neptune and Amphitrite, c. 1688
Oil on canvas, 31³⁄₈ x 40¹⁄₂
Gifts of Mr. & Mrs. S. Kendrick Guernsey

AG 1972.16.1

Charles Joseph Natoire, French, 1700–1777
The Awakening of Venus, 1741
Oil on canvas, 38³/₄ x 49¹/₄
Signed and dated at left: *Natoire f/1741*
Museum purchase with funds provided by the Morton R.
Hirschberg Memorial Fund & the Cummer Council

AP 1991.5.1

As a student at the French Royal Academy of Painting
and Sculpture, Charles Natoire was awarded the coveted
Grand Prix de Rome in 1721. After studying in Italy from
1723 to 1729, Natoire returned to France and was elected to membership in the Academy in 1734. Known for
his expert draftsmanship and fine history paintings,
Natoire executed numerous decorative commissions for
the French royalty and nobility. Natoire returned to
Rome in 1751 to serve as Director of the French
Academy, a position he held until his retirement twenty-
three years later.

This painting was originally part of an elaborately
decorated interior and was set into a paneled wall.
The awakening and adornment of Venus by her
attendants, the Three Graces, was a popular subject
because of its mythological and literary associations.
The theme also provided an acceptable vehicle for the
inclusion of the light, often sensuous subject matter
associated with the Rococo style. Red roses are included
as an attribute of the goddess. The two *putti,* symbolic of
profane and sacred love, may represent Venus's sons
Eros, commonly referred to as Cupid, and Anteros.

39

Philipp Jakob Straub, Austrian, 1706–1774
St. Longinus, c. 1760
Limewood, gilt and polychromed, 56
Gift of Mrs. Genevieve Schultz Ayers

AG 1981.8.1

In European churches, one frequently finds sculptural ensembles that depict important events from the life of Christ. This robed saint dressed as a Roman soldier was originally one element of a sculptural group representing the crucifixion of Christ. According to the Gospel of St. John, after Christ died on the cross, "one of the soldiers pierced his side with a spear, and at once there came out blood and water" (John 19:34). The soldier was not identified in the Bible, but was later given the name Longinus. The story was elaborated in the *Golden Legend* (c. 1275), a popular collection of tales and legends written by the Italian author Jacopo da Voragine. According to his version, the Roman soldier was suffering from an eye ailment at the time of Christ's crucifixion. After rubbing the blood in his eyes that had spilled from Christ's wound, Longinus's eyesight miraculously improved, and the Roman soldier converted to the Christian faith.

Philipp Jakob Straub, a member of an established family of woodcarvers and cabinetmakers, was born in Wiesensteig in southeastern Germany. After being trained by his father, he worked in Munich and Vienna in various workshops. He settled in the Austrian city of Graz in 1733 and married the widow of a local sculptor. That year Straub took over her deceased husband's workshop and became the city's most important sculptor.

40

Jan ten Compe, Dutch, 1713–1761
View of Nieuwmarkt, Amsterdam, 1752
Oil on panel, 21⁵/₁₆ x 29 ³/₈
Signed: *J Ten Compe f.*
Museum purchase with membership contributions

AP 1963.6.1

Raised and educated in the orphanage of the Reformed
Church in Amsterdam, Jan ten Compe found his calling
in painting views of major Dutch towns. His paintings
are so precise that they are of special interest to
historians because of their topographic and
architectural accuracy. He frequently rendered famous
buildings in minute detail and added daily activities
to enliven the scene. Popular as a painter and successful
as an art dealer, ten Compe was highly regarded
by his contemporaries.

Bathed in morning sunlight, the turreted building
dominates Nieuwmarkt Square in Amsterdam.
Originally built as a gate in a series of defensive
bulwarks surrounding the city, the stately structure
became a "Waag," or weigh house, in the seventeenth
century. A small group of men load several large bags
onto a scale in front of the weigh house,
while a boy flies his kite in the square.
The skeleton painted on one of the doors of the weigh
house indicates the entrance to the meeting room of the
Amsterdam Guild of Surgeons.

Alexander Roslin, Swedish, 1718–1793
Henriette Begouen, 1790
Oil on canvas, 23¹/₄ x 19¹/₂
Signed and dated lower left: *le Chevl Roslin 1790*
Museum purchase with membership contributions

AP 1968.10.1

Alexander Roslin left his native Sweden in 1745 to work
in northern Italy before settling in Paris in 1752. He was
accepted into the Royal Academy of Painting and
Sculpture the following year. Acclaimed for his portraiture
and the ability to render the most delicate fabrics, Roslin's
commissions included portraits of Catherine the Great
(1729–1796) of Russia and the daughters of Louis XV
(1710–1774) of France. In honor of his artistic achievements, Roslin received a Swedish knighthood in 1773.

This portrait was first exhibited in Paris at the 1791
Salon as *Young Girl Holding Flowers.* In 1797, Henriette
Begouen (1780–1825), the sitter for this portrait, married
Martin Foäche, the son of a prominent family in Le
Havre who were patrons of Roslin. The garland and
bouquet associate her with Flora, the Roman goddess of
flowers. The simple costume and floral motifs suggest
the idyllic, rural lifestyle idealized by many of the French
aristocracy during the early and middle eighteenth
century. The aging Roslin executed this portrait in the
lighthearted mood and pastel palette of the somewhat
outdated Rococo style, which by 1790 was rapidly being
replaced by a reserved classical style, more in keeping
with the spirit of the time.

Marie Victoire Lemoine, French, 1754–1820
Louis Benoît Zamor, 1785
Oil on canvas, 25⅝ x 21½
Signed and dated lower right:
Lemoine pinxit / Paris Mars 1785
Museum purchase with Council funds

AP 1994.3.1

Traditionally attributed to the portrait painter Jacques Antoine Marie Lemoine (1751–1824), this work is now associated with a successful female artist of the period, Marie Victoire Lemoine. At a time when the artistic education of females was limited by their exclusion from studies of nude models, Lemoine concentrated on the production of finely detailed portraits, miniatures, and genre subjects. She was born to a middle-class family in Paris and had three sisters, two of whom became professional artists. Though her sisters married, Marie Victoire concentrated on her career and remained single throughout her lifetime. She exhibited at the Salon of the French Academy between 1796 and 1814.

The youthful subject of this portrait has been identified as the notorious Louis Benoît Zamor, protégé of Louis XV's (1710–1774) mistress, Madame Du Barry (1743–1793). After Du Barry expelled Zamor from her home for sympathizing with the French Revolution, he joined the Committee of Public Safety. His testimony against his former patroness was a contributing factor in her execution by guillotine in 1793. The sitter's identification is difficult to confirm because eighteenth-century accounts variously describe Zamor as being of either Bengali or African descent and differ regarding his age. In any case, Lemoine created a vivid likeness of this youth, whose elegant satin attire and embroidered vest indicate his connection with a noble family.

43

Cornelis van Spaendonck,
Dutch, 1756–1840
Still Life with Flowers and a Bas-relief, c. 1793
Oil on canvas, 32 x 25½
Bequest of Ninah M. H. Cummer

C 163.1

Still life emerged as an independent category of painting in the Netherlands during the late sixteenth and seventeenth centuries. A century later, French patrons' fascination with earlier Dutch works enabled the artist Cornelis van Spaendonck to find a ready audience for his still life imagery when he moved to France. In 1773, he joined his elder brother and teacher Gerard (1746–1822) in Paris and served as his collaborator. From 1785 to 1800 Cornelis was Director of the Sèvres porcelain factory. He was admitted to the French Academy of Painting and Sculpture in 1789 and exhibited his flower paintings regularly in Paris at the Salon until 1833.

The varied surfaces and textures rendered in this composition demonstrate van Spaendonck's technical virtuosity. An alabaster vase overflowing with flowers, including a tulip, rose, peony, and hyacinth, rests upon a platform decorated with a classical relief carving. The crystal bowl of fruit contains a pomegranate, a traditional Christian symbol of the Resurrection. Allusions to the transience of life are found in the decaying flower in the foreground and the skillfully executed drops of dew upon the leaves.

44

Sir Henry Raeburn, Scottish, 1756–1823
Lady Harriet Don with Her Son, c. 1800
Oil on canvas, 35³/₄ x 27³/₄
Bequest of Ninah M. H. Cummer

C 142.1

Henry Raeburn, orphaned at a very early age, was
apprenticed to a jeweler and a miniaturist in Edinburgh
when he was sixteen. He became the most renowned of
all Scottish painters of his generation, although he had
no professional training as an artist. Raeburn spent his
artistic career in Edinburgh working almost exclusively
on portraits, though he did make an artistic trip to Italy
where he visited Rome for more than a year. His return
trip to Scotland in late 1785 was made by way of visits
to various major European cities including London and
Paris. After much success as a portrait painter, he was
elected to the Royal Academy in London in 1815 and
was knighted in 1822 by George IV (1762–1830).

Raeburn developed a highly original style based on direct
observation of his sitters. He was particularly adept at
combining loose rapid brushwork with remarkably
precise detail. He also used dramatic light to give his
sitters immediacy and presence. All of Raeburn's best
qualities of portraiture can be seen in this painting of
Lady Don and her son Alexander (later Sir Alexander Don).

45

Paul Storr, English, 1771–1844
Teakettle with detachable urn, 1832
Silver, 13
Gift of Mrs. Winthrop Bancroft

AG 1996.1.1

Paul Storr was one of the most celebrated artists in the
history of English silver, creating works for many
aristocratic patrons including the future King George
IV (1762–1830). Storr grew up around the tools of the
silver making trade because his father was a silver
chaser, or someone who ornamented silver vessels.
After a seven-year apprenticeship in London, Storr
began an independent career, submitting his first mark
to the Goldsmiths' Guild in 1793. From 1807 through
1838, Storr entered into partnerships with several of
London's leading silversmiths, all the while
strengthening his independent reputation.

During the early nineteenth century, England experienced great prosperity, effecting a dramatic rise in the
production of luxury items made of silver. The preferred
style for silver design during this period was a combination of elegant classical forms and extravagant surface
decoration. This teakettle was created during Storr's
highly successful partnership with John Mortimer (active
until 1836/42). Storr's love of organic ornamentation
can be seen in the richly embossed floral sprays and
winding foliage that envelop the handle, spout, and
stand. The upper body of this simply shaped teakettle is
adorned with a delicate garland of flowers and leaves.
The inscribed coat of arms, as yet unidentified, and
Latin motto *Fac et Spera* ("Do and Hope") indicate the
teakettle was part of a commissioned set.

46

Carl Friedrich Heinrich Werner,
German, 1808–1894
The Colossi of Memnon, 1866
Watercolor on paper, 37$\frac{1}{2}$ x 22$\frac{1}{2}$
Signed and dated lower right: *C. Werner f. 1866*
Gift of Joseph Jeffers Dodge

AG 1996.2.65

Travel to Egypt and the Holy Land became popular in the
nineteenth century. In addition to scholars, adventurers,
and an emerging class of tourists, many artists traveled to
archaeological sites in the Middle East and elsewhere to
record their impressions of ancient temples and Pharaonic
monuments. In this very precise artistic rendering, the two
seated statues of Pharaoh Amenhotep III (1408–1372 B.C.),
known as the Colossi of Memnon, tower above small
groups of visitors. These sculptures rise to a height of
sixty-four feet, and were erected in the valley of Deir-el-
Bahri near Thebes, c. 1380 B.C. In the background, other
ruins such as the funerary temple of King Rameses II
(1301–1235 B.C.) and the temple of Queen Hatshepsut
can be discerned. (1511–1480 B.C.)

The German artist Carl Werner frequently traveled to
Rome, Greece, and Spain, and visited Palestine and
Egypt in 1864. His work is admired for its topographic
and archaeological exactitude. He received his artistic
training in Dresden and Munich. For many years Werner
was a professor of art in Leipzig.

Emil (Niels Emil Severin) Holm,
Danish, 1823–1863
Greek Amphitheater at Taormina, Sicily, 1858
Oil on canvas, 31³/₈ x 48
Signed and dated lower left:
N Emil Holm Messina 1858
Gift of Joseph Jeffers Dodge

AG 1966.2.64

A woman appears to be picking berries or flowers on
the steep hillside, while a small number of visitors are
seen exploring the ruins of the amphitheater in
Taormina near Messina on the island of Sicily. Except
for the stage and adjacent buildings, the theater hewn in
the rock is of Greek origin, but was reconstructed during
Roman and later times. Beyond the ruins, the town of
Taormina can be seen with its church San Pancrazio.
An ancient citadel crowns the hills on the right.
The view from the site is exceptionally beautiful, with
the volcanic Mount Etna dominating the surrounding
mountains. To the north, the rugged outlines of the
coast and the mountains of Calabria across the sea
make up one of the most famous sceneries in the world.

Taormina was a favorite European winter resort in the
nineteenth century. The Danish artist Emil Holm moved
there in 1857 only returning to Denmark shortly before
his death. As a young man, Holm frequented the
Drawing Academy in his native Aarhus before entering
the Academy of Fine Arts in Copenhagen. He was given
several important Academy awards in 1844 and 1854.
His depictions of landscapes in and around Taormina
are particularly noteworthy.

48

Félix Barrias, French, 1822–1907
Life Class in a Paris Studio, 1869
Oil on canvas, 15¹³/₁₆ x 13⁷/₈
Signed and dated lower right: *F Barrias 1869*
Museum purchase with membership contributions

AP 1963.3.1

In this sketch of a typical art class, the viewer's gaze is drawn to the back of a nude female model, while eight young artists observe and paint her. This classically shaped model adopts a characteristic *contrapposto* stance, leaning on her left leg, thereby pushing her right hip outward. The young artist at the bottom right has been tentatively identified as Edgar Degas (1834–1917), who was a student under Barrias for a short time. A number of small, framed pictures hang high on the back wall of the studio representing a possible sampling of student work.

Félix Barrias won the Grand Prix de Rome at the age of twenty-two and was a regular exhibitor at the Paris Salon for more than sixty years. A champion of academicism in painting, he was known for his flawless technique and predictable palette. In addition to easel paintings, he executed many large scale mural decorations, both religious and secular, in public buildings such as the Hôtel de Ville in Paris, the Musée Picardie in Amiens, and the Argentine Pavilion at the Paris World Fair of 1889.

49

William-Adolphe Bouguereau,
French, 1825–1905
Return from the Harvest, 1878
Oil on canvas, 95 x 67
Signed and dated lower left: *W. Bouguereau. 1878*
Museum purchase with membership contributions

AP 1964.2.1

After a strict academic training as a painter at the Ecole des Beaux–Arts in Paris, Bouguereau was awarded the prestigious Prix de Rome in 1850. This prize enabled him to move to Rome, where he industriously studied and copied the Italian masters. Four years later, Bouguereau returned to Paris. His extraordinary success as a painter, combined with his influence as a teacher, make him one of the masters of nineteenth-century academic painting. As a prominent juror, Bouguereau also exerted decisive influence over the annual Paris Salon, keeping it within the bounds of official academicism and systematically rejecting the experimental painting of Edouard Manet (1832–1883) and the Impressionists.

The donkey ride, featured prominently in this painting, offers Bouguereau the opportunity to show his astounding technical skills and classical learning in the representation of an age-old harvest festival. The child riding the donkey is playing the role of the Roman god Bacchus, accompanied by joyful peasants. Additionally, the theme of this painting carries Biblical allusions whereby the child is identified as the young Christ. This painting was commissioned by Alexander T. Stewart, a wealthy American department store owner of Irish descent, who stipulated that "the painting was to be the artist's greatest work and not a nude subject." Unfortunately, Stewart died before Bouguereau could finish this much admired painting.

50

Gustave Léonard de Jonghe, Belgian, 1829–1893
The Japanese Fan, c. 1865
Oil on canvas, 44¼ x 34¹/₁₆
Gift of Francis & Miranda Childress Foundation

AG 1988.3.1

In 1855, Gustave de Jonghe moved from Belgium to
Paris and exhibited regularly in the Salon for the next
thirty years. He returned to Brussels in 1882 after being
struck with paralysis and blindness. De Jonghe was
particularly famous for his portraits of women and
family scenes. The artist had an uncanny ability to
represent elegant and sumptuous interiors, which seem
quiet and unassuming on the surface, but which hint at
underlying passion and seduction. This bourgeois
lightheartedness is often interpreted as typical of the
French Second Empire. The women seem to languish
in dreams, surrounded by exotic elements.

The Japanese fan, so prominently featured in the title, is
merely a small object on the floor. The dramatic tension
radiates from the confrontation between the bird and
the young woman and is further reinforced by the chaos
of the room. It is uncertain whether the woman is
disciplining the cockatoo or the bird is threatening her.
The violent scene in the Japanese screen behind her
reinforces the impression of a conflict between two
antagonists. The prevalence of oriental objects
and subjects in de Jonghe's painting reflects the late
nineteenth-century fascination with Japanese art
and aesthetics, a phenonemon called *Japonisme*,
which was spawned by the newly opened trade
routes between Europe, the United States, and Japan.

51

Paul Camille Guigou, French, 1834–1871
The Mouth of the Lourmarin River, 1867
Oil on canvas, 28⅛ x 46⅛
Signed and dated lower left: *Paul Guigou 67*
Morton R. Hirschberg Memorial Fund

AP 1989.16.1

Paul Guigou did not start painting full time until he reached the age of twenty-seven, after working as a notary in Apt and Marseille. He died only ten years later. In that relatively short span, he produced approximately 400 paintings, which are almost exclusively views of the natural environment of his beloved native Provence. In mid-nineteenth-century France, many writers and artists feared that the natural beauty, traditions, and language of Provence (*la langue d'oc*) were being threatened by an increasingly centralized French bureaucracy. Guigou, as well as other writers and artists, was active in this nationalistic movement for the preservation of this beautiful part of France.

Guigou's style of painting bridges the interests of the Barbizon School of artists with the emerging Impressionist painters, all of whom championed open air painting. His keen interest in identifiable locations resulted in paintings of panoramic views rendered in broad brushstrokes and lively colors. This painting was exhibited in the Paris Salon of 1868 and received favorable notes in the artistic press.

52

Louis Valtat, French, 1869–1952
Valtat and His Son
Oil on canvas, 23¾ x 29¼
Signed lower right: *L.V.*
Gift of Mr. & Mrs. Edward W. Lane, Jr.

AG 1989.12.1

This engaging double portrait shows a painter, brush in hand, in front of an easel, accompanied by a young boy. It is a self-portrait of the artist Louis Valtat; the young boy is his son. Born in Dieppe in northwestern France and raised in Versailles, Valtat spent considerable time in the South of France. He was acquainted with many artists living in Provence and was a personal friend of Auguste Renoir. Valtat's activities as a stage designer remain a little explored aspect of his artistic career.

Valtat's relative obscurity has been attributed to a lack of aggressive marketing by his dealer, the well-known Ambroise Vollard (1867–1939). Valtat, however, was active at the crossroads of various art styles, demonstrating an interest in new and innovative approaches such as Pointillism. As an artist, Valtat was interested in the scientific study of light. Later in life he was associated with the Fauves, a group of artists known for their loose handling of the brush.

André Lhote, French, 1885–1962
Cubist Nude, 1917
Oil on canvas, 35³/₈ x 25
Signed upper left: *A. Lhote*
Morton R. Hirschberg Memorial Fund

AP 1986.2.1

The subject, a powerful female nude, her hands held
behind her back, has been transformed into a mosaic of
refracted planes and subtle neutral colors. The reduction
of the woman's body to a formula of solid, geometric
simplicity makes the painting a representative example
of Analytic Cubism, one of the most widely influential
avant-garde movements of the twentieth century. Space
and recognizable objects, in this instance the female
body, remained important in Cubist art. Cubist aesthetic
theory paid homage to the forces of change, speed,
spatial relativity, and the machine, which were gathering
momentum in Europe prior to World War I.

André Lhote was born in Bordeaux and was trained by
his father as a woodcarver. Lhote moved to Paris when
he was twenty-five. He served as a professor in several
art academies from 1918 until 1922, when he founded
his own academy on the rue d'Odessa. Prolific as a writer
and art critic, he published two influential works, *Treatise
on Landscape Painting*, 1939, and *Treatise on Figure
Painting*, 1950. Lhote was highly influential on an
international level and lectured widely outside of France.

54

Pablo Picasso, Spanish, 1881–1973
Nude Seated Before a Curtain,
from the *Vollard Suite,* 1931
Etching on paper, 11¾ x 8¾
Museum purchase

AP 1965.27.1

A renewed interest in naturalistically rendered, classically
inspired figures characterizes the painting, sculpture, and
graphic work of Pablo Picasso executed in the 1920s and
1930s. The suite of etchings dealing with the theme of
The Sculptor's Studio is particularly striking. In this series
of etchings Picasso explores the visual possibilities of the
sculptor and his model, inspired by his newly initiated
relationship with Marie-Therese Walter, at that time a
twenty-one year old German woman. The artist is
represented as lover, active creator, or more often,
a melancholy, pensive observer, looking contemplatively
at his model and muse in these lyrically accomplished
prints. *The Sculptor's Studio*, done in 1933, formed a
subsection of 46 of a total of 100 copperplates created
between 1931 and 1936, which were acquired by
Picasso's dealer Ambroise Vollard (1867–1939). They
were printed in Paris by Roger Lacourière before Vollard's
death in 1939, but not offered for sale until 1950.

Pablo Picasso, a protean figure in the history of
twentieth-century art, was born in Malaga, Spain.
Immensely productive, Picasso's influence was
particularly felt in his decisive contributions to
the forging of Cubism, and generally speaking, to the
development of the image of the modern artist.
The seated nude from the *Vollard Suite* shows the
influence of Rome and classical culture on Picasso's art.
A sense of grandeur permeates his paintings and prints
from this period, notably in his portrayal of the female
body, inspired by the majestic stone sculptures of
muscular warriors and draped goddesses that he had
seen in Rome in 1917.

55

Marie Laurencin, French, 1885–1956
Woman with Guitar, 1943
Oil on canvas, 25³/₄ x 21¹/₂
Signed and dated upper right:
Marie Laurencin 1943
Gift of Jack & Marcelle Bear in honor of John S. Bunker

AG 1995.2.1

Poet and painter Marie Laurencin was closely associated
with the Parisian avant-garde movement. Beginning in
1907, Laurencin was muse and companion to the famed
poet and critic Guillaume Apollinaire (1880–1918) and
was featured in many of his writings. She exhibited
seven canvases in the revolutionary 1913 Armory Show
in New York, a landmark exhibition in the history of
Modern art. Forced into exile by the outbreak of World
War I, she moved to Spain in 1914, but returned to Paris
in 1921. Following her resettlement in Paris, Laurencin
established herself as a leading society portraitist, book
illustrator, and costume and textile designer. Her
costume designs and stage sets for the Ballets Russes'
presentation of Sergei Diaghilev's (1872–1929) *Les Biches*
in 1924 met with great success.

Woman with Guitar demonstrates Laurencin's schematic
treatment of human anatomy. The sitter's porcelain skin,
demure mouth, and widely set almond eyes are
particularly striking. These stylistic elements were partly
based on her knowledge of the arts of Africa. The color
scheme is typical of her paintings, in which flat planes
of pastel hues predominate. Laurencin achieves an
ephemeral elegance with her unique combination of
simplified forms, graceful lines, and pleasing palette.
Reflecting her own interest in the literary, performing,
and visual arts, Laurencin often painted figures in the
guise of the Muses, draped in togas and carrying the
attributes of their art.

56

THE AMERICAN COLLECTION

Benjamin West, American, 1738–1820

The Honorable Mrs. Shute Barrington, 1808

Oil on canvas, 50¹/₈ x 40³/₁₆

Signed and dated lower left: *B. West. 1808*

Foundation purchase

AP 1960.2.1

Benjamin West was born in Pennsylvania and achieved success as a portrait painter before moving to Italy in 1760. After three years of study, primarily in Rome, West relocated to London where he received international recognition as a history painter. In an era when many American artists were traveling to Europe for training, West became firmly established in London as a master painter and teacher. In 1768, he became a founding member of the Royal Academy and in 1792 was elected president of that prestigious organization. West was appointed Historical Painter to George III (1738–1820) in the year 1772.

The subject of this portrait is Jane Barrington (1733–1807), who married the Right Reverend The Honorable Shute Barrington (1734–1826), bishop of Llandaff in 1770. Both the Reverend and Mrs. Barrington are called "The Honorable" because the Reverend was the younger son of a viscount. The Bible upon which Mrs. Barrington leans and the image of Durham Cathedral in the background allude to the couple's service to the church. After leaving Llandaff, her husband served as bishop of Salisbury (1782–1791) and bishop of Durham (1791–1826). Dated one year after Mrs. Barrington's death, the work seems to be a posthumous portrait commissioned by the bishop. It most likely served as a companion to a portrait of the bishop that is now at Merton College, Oxford.

57

Gilbert Stuart, American, 1755–1828
Samuel Williams, Esq., c. 1808
Oil on panel, 26¼ x 21¼
Gift of the John C. Myers, Sr. family

AG 1959.1.1

Early in Gilbert Stuart's career, he limned portraits in Newport, Rhode Island before beginning his formal artistic training. Moving to London in 1775, he entered the studio of Benjamin West (1738–1820), another American artist active in England. In 1787, Stuart exhibited a full-length portrait at the Royal Academy and gained serious recognition in the press. After eighteen years abroad, he returned to America and painted portraits of leading citizens while he worked in New York, Philadelphia, and Washington, D.C. He finally settled in Boston in 1805. His peers deemed him the father of American portraiture. Stuart is best known for his portraits of George Washington, one of which appears on the American dollar bill.

Samuel Williams (1769–1813), a scion of the prominent Williams family in Boston, appears to have been a wealthy merchant who owned property in and around Baltimore. He was a direct descendent of one of the signers of the Declaration of Independence and of the benefactors of Williams College in Williamstown, Massachusetts.
This work is one of a group of fifteen portraits Stuart painted of the Williams family between 1793 and 1819. The portrait illustrates Stuart's characteristic rapid execution and ability to paint a strong likeness.

58

Thomas Sully, American, 1783–1872
Captain Samuel Worthington Dewey, 1834
Oil on canvas, 30^{1}/$_{16}$ x 24^{7}/$_{8}$
Gift of Mr. & Mrs. Stanley Bernstein

AG 1998.3.1

An American painter born in England, Thomas Sully and his family, who were circus performers, moved to America in 1792. In 1807 he went to Boston and met Gilbert Stuart (1755–1828) before settling in Philadelphia. On two occasions, Sully returned to England where he received encouragement from the painter Benjamin West (1738–1820). Sully became a very successful portrait painter and attracted clients throughout New England.

A Philadelphia druggist commissioned this portrait of Captain Dewey, who had recently attracted national attention. In the summer of 1834, when the American frigate *Constitution*, commonly known as *Old Ironsides*, was being repaired in the Charleston Navy Yard near Boston, a figurehead depicting President Andrew Jackson (1767–1845) was installed upon the ship. Jackson was unpopular in the financial centers of the Northeast because of his economic reform program and stringent monetary policy, and Boston was no exception. One evening, a young captain rowed out to the *Constitution* and sawed off Jackson's head. Much of Boston applauded this brazen act of partisanship. Captain Dewey became a folk hero in the Northeast and a man much maligned by the supporters of President Jackson.

59

John James Audubon, American, 1785–1851
Florida Rats (Neotoma Floridana),
Male, Female and Young, 1841
Pencil, ink, and watercolor on paper, 21³/₈ x 17³/₈
Signed and dated lower right: *JJA Novr. 30th 1841*
Museum purchase with membership contributions

AP 1966.11.1

Born in Haiti and raised in France, John James Audubon became interested in natural science and art as a child. He moved to America in 1803 to oversee an estate outside of Philadelphia that was owned by his father, but instead spent most of his time drawing birds. After traveling extensively throughout the country drawing and painting numerous species of birds, Audubon returned to Philadelphia in an attempt to publish his works. His paintings met with a disappointing reception and Audubon left for England, where he successfully exhibited his work.

In 1826, Audubon began the project to publish his renowned *The Birds of America*. The first edition was completed in four volumes in 1839, and was later expanded to seven volumes. In late 1839, he enlisted the help of Rev. John Bachman, head of the Lutheran Church in Charleston and a noted naturalist, to write the text for his new project illustrating American mammals. This watercolor of Florida rats is Audubon's original study for plate IV of *The Viviparous Quadrupeds of North America* that was published between 1846 and 1854. On this drawing the detailed instructions in Audubon's handwriting indicate to the printmaker how to execute the lithograph for publication

60

John Neagle, American, 1796–1865
The Dickson Brothers, c. 1840
Oil on canvas, 29 x 36¹/₈
Gift of the John C. Myers, Sr. family

AG 1966.32.1

John Neagle received his artistic training and spent most of his life in Philadelphia. He dominated the art of portraiture in that city along with his friend and father-in-law, Thomas Sully (1783–1872). Neagle spent some time in Boston studying the work of the renowned Gilbert Stuart (1755–1828), whose portrait style had a lasting influence on him.

This painting is a subtle family portrait. The four young boys seated around the table are the children of Neagle's cousin John Dickson and are Robert, Levi, John Jr., and James. The boys' parents are humorously depicted as stick figure drawings on the paper that hangs off the tabletop in the foreground. The children's favored possessions are carefully placed on the table. The watch sitting on top of the drawing of the parents symbolizes the fleeting passage of the boys' childhood.

61

George P. A. Healy, American, 1813–1894
Portrait of Andrew Jackson, 1845
Oil on canvas, 30^1/$_{16}$ x 25^1/$_4$
Signed and dated middle right: *Healy 1845*
Gift of Mr. & Mrs. Algur Meadows, Dallas, Texas

AG 1972.14.1

In the spring of 1845, King Louis-Philippe of France (1773–1850) heard that Old Hickory, President Andrew Jackson (1767–1845), was dying. The king quickly dispatched George Healy to paint the famous president's portrait at his home in Tennessee. At first, the ailing Jackson refused to sit for Healy. The artist's diplomatic persistence prevailed, however, and "somehow Healy managed to push his brush a hair's breadth ahead of the Reaper's scythe," as observed by a curator at the National Portrait Gallery in Washington, D.C. in a recent publication. Jackson died on June 8, 1845, just days after Healy finished his portrait. The Cummer picture is one of three known copies of the artist's painting made for Louis-Philippe and is the version Healy painted for himself.

Healy was a precocious young American artist who received little formal artistic training. Nevertheless, he opened studios in Boston and Paris before he turned twenty-three. In 1839 he came to the attention of King Louis-Philippe and soon was executing royal commissions. Healy later returned to America and settled in Chicago in 1856. He became the leading artist in the Midwest and painted hundreds of portraits of Americans, including presidents, statesmen, and leading citizens. Healy moved back to Europe in 1864, frequently traveling to his native country. He made the last of his thirty crossings in 1892 when he finally settled in Chicago.

62

John Frederick Kensett, American, 1816–1872
Marine View of Beacon Rock, Newport Harbor, 1864
Oil on canvas, 28½ x 45¾
Signed and dated lower right: *JFK '64*
Bequest of Ninah M. H. Cummer

C 157.1

Trained by his English father as an engraver, John
Kensett chose to become a painter. In 1840 he went to
Europe for several years to study Old Master paintings
and to develop his skills in London, Paris, and Rome.
Upon his return to America, Kensett was recognized for
his excellence in landscape painting and was elected to
the National Academy of Design in New York. Kensett
was also one of the founders of The Metropolitan
Museum of Art in New York in 1870.

This painting illustrates Kensett's switch from painting
mountains and woodland interiors to coastal views.
It also marks a change in his style to more
contemplative painting known as Luminism, which
focused on nuances of light and atmosphere, a method
that may have been influenced by the new medium of
photography. Kensett painted this favored panorama of
Newport Harbor in Rhode Island several times.
The viewer looks across Brenton Cove toward Beacon
Rock on the right and Fort Adams on the left in the
distance. This painting is renowned for its indelible
sense of calmness, clarity, and quiet, and occupies a
central position in Kensett's oeuvre. Characteristic of his
mature Luminist style, this work contains a sense of
balance, spareness, and a rich evocation of hues.

63

Martin Johnson Heade, American, 1819–1904
Orchid with an Amethyst Hummingbird, c. 1870
Oil on canvas, 18$^1/_{16}$ x 10$^1/_8$
Signed lower left: *MJ Heade*
Bequest of Ninah M. H. Cummer

C 112.1

Martin Johnson Heade has acquired a reputation both
as an artist and a naturalist. His studies of nature,
particularly of hummingbirds, began in his youth and
continued throughout his life. Following in the footsteps
of other American artists, Heade went to South America
and the Caribbean between 1863 and 1870. He visited
Brazil, Nicaragua, Colombia, Puerto Rico, and Jamaica.
At the age of sixty-four, Heade married and moved from
New York to St. Augustine, Florida, where he continued
to paint for many years. Heade's patron at the time was
Henry Flagler (1830–1913), railroad magnate and real
estate developer of Florida's east coast. When Flagler
built the great Hotel Ponce de León in 1885 (now Flagler
College), he included studios for artists in order to
attract them to St. Augustine. Heade occupied one
of these studios.

Heade's writings on the conservation of Florida's natural
wilderness are unparalleled as pioneering efforts.
Heade's contribution to American nineteenth-century
painting is embodied by his study of light, particularly as
reflected in paintings of sun-dappled fields and marshes.
In this painting, the orchid is a carefully studied
representation of the *Cattleya labiata Lindley,* which is
found in Venezuela, whereas the hummingbird has been
identified as an Amethyst hummingbird, commonly
found in the Amazon Basin.

64

Eastman Johnson, American, 1824–1906
Kitchen at Mount Vernon, c. 1857
Oil on panel, 12⁹/₁₆ x 20⁹/₁₆
Signed at lower left: *EJ*
Bequest of Ninah M. H. Cummer

C 117.1

Eastman Johnson was born in Lovell, Maine and studied printmaking in Boston for two years. In 1845 the artist moved to Washington, D.C., where he made portrait drawings of prominent citizens including Dolley Madison (1768–1849) and John Quincy Adams (1767–1848). Johnson began a two-year study of painting at the Düsseldorf Academy in 1848. He then traveled to The Hague and studied Dutch seventeenth-century painting for three years. After visiting Paris, Johnson returned to America and settled in New York. Johnson is well known for his genre scenes and images of African Americans, particularly those painted during the Civil War (1861–1865).

In 1857 Johnson visited Mount Vernon, the Virginia home of George Washington (1732–1799). The artist was related by marriage to the Washington descendent who owned the estate. The home had fallen into a state of disrepair and neglect, which by 1858 motivated a group of women to organize the Mount Vernon Ladies Association to purchase and renovate the property. Johnson painted three known versions of this interior scene, depicting an unknown woman and three children in a dilapidated plantation kitchen. The quiet domesticity depicted here is reminiscent of Dutch genre paintings Johnson knew from his studies, but the specific subject choice is distinctly that of an artist concerned with chronicling contemporary American life.

65

George Inness, American, 1825–1894
Perugia, 1870
Oil on canvas, 13⅛ x 10
Signed and dated lower left:
G. Inness Perugia 1870
Bequest of Ninah M. H. Cummer

C 195.1

George Inness was born in Newburgh, New York, the
fifth of thirteen children. He left the family grocery
business and decided on a career in art at an early age.
He received little formal training, but by the age of
twenty was exhibiting at the National Academy of
Design in New York. Between 1851 and 1875 Inness
traveled to Europe and spent much of his time in Italy
and France. In an attempt to relieve his epileptic
symptoms, Inness sought the serenity of rural
Massachusetts. The restless artist continued to travel
between Europe and his studio in Tarpon Springs,
Florida, making his final home in Montclair, New Jersey.
Inness never associated himself closely with one
artistic style or movement, but created individualized
paintings of civilized landscapes infused with a sense
of the divine.

This work was painted during Inness's second sojourn
in Italy from 1870 to 1874. In the late 1860s he became
a member of the Raritan Bay Union utopian community
and started to study spiritualism. The teachings of the
Swedish mystic Emanuel Swedenborg (1688–1772), who
claimed that all material objects were spiritually
charged, became especially important to Inness. From
then on he produced landscapes based on his religious
beliefs. Rather than painting nature as a topographic
reality, Inness concentrated on capturing a harmonious
and expressive vision. In this painting, the hazy veil of
golden light evokes the mystery and beauty of the Italian
countryside near the ancient Etruscan town of Perugia.

Herman Herzog, German/American, 1832–1932
Figure in a River Landscape, c. 1910
Oil on canvas, 15^{13}/$_{16}$ x 19^{7}/$_{8}$
Signed lower left: *H. Herzog*
Gift of Mr. & Mrs. C. Herman Terry

AG 1987.11.1

A native of the German city of Bremen, Herman Herzog
entered the Düsseldorf Academy in Westphalia when he
was seventeen. The young artist was attracted to
landscape compositions and traveled to Norway, Italy,
and Holland in pursuit of inspiration. Herzog enjoyed
critical acclaim, receiving an honorable mention from
the Paris Salon in 1864. During the 1860s, the artist
moved his family to the United States for both political
and artistic reasons. Herzog settled in Philadelphia
but traveled widely from Maine to Mexico, exploring
the almost limitless vistas his adopted country offered
his artistic eye.

Between 1885 and 1910, Herzog made regular visits to
his son's home in Gainesville, Florida. The lush
vegetation between the Suwannee and Homossassa
Rivers appealed to the artist's taste for quiet drama,
and Herzog created more than 250 Florida views.
In this example, a loose brushstroke and a keen interest
in atmospheric effects are evident. The heavy
application of paint in the palm trees contrasts with the
much lighter touch in the overcast sky. The artist's
preoccupation with the transient effects of light later
manifested itself in an interest in photography.
This painted record of unspoiled Florida was created for
Herzog's appreciation alone without any audience in
mind. Financial success allowed the artist to cease
selling his paintings later in life, resulting in a studio
collection of nearly one thousand works at the time
of his death.

67

James McNeill Whistler, American, 1834–1903
Street in Bourges, France, 1897–99
Watercolor with touches of gouache on paper,
8$\frac{1}{2}$ x 5$\frac{1}{8}$
Bequest of Ninah M. H. Cummer

C 197.1

James McNeill Whistler was born in America, but his
family settled in England where the young artist attended
lectures at the Royal Academy in London. After a brief
return to the United States, he went back to Europe at
the age of twenty-one, determined to make a career as
an artist. Whistler enrolled at the Ecole Impériale et
Spéciale de Dessin in Paris. He became well established
as a painter and acted as an important link between the
avant-garde artists of Europe and America. This mercurial
artist developed a reputation as painter, printmaker,
writer, critic, and society figure, and is acknowledged as
one of the masters of etching in the history of art.

At the end of his long and distinguished career, Whistler
spent the summers in France painting simple street
scenes and small seascapes. This diminutive painting is
highly characteristic of his watercolors from the late
1890s, both in subject matter and technique. Whistler
typically jotted little sketches from his travels by painting
thinly on brown paper. In these painted snapshots, he
outlined the subject in brush then quickly added light
washes of color. Whistler often let the paper show
through to suggest light or texture in his compositions.
The dominant frame with gilt and deep moulding is
characteristic of Whistler's interest in the presentation
of his creations.

68

William Stanley Haseltine, American, 1835–1900
Sunset on the Grand Canal, Venice, early 1870s
Oil on canvas, 14 x 25
Gift of Helen Haseltine Plowden through the National
Academy of Design, New York

AG 1961.7.1

William Haseltine came from a Philadelphia family firmly
associated with the arts. One brother was a successful
sculptor and the other was an art dealer. William was
educated at the University of Pennsylvania and at
Harvard University. He was apprenticed to a
Philadelphia artist before traveling abroad to study at
the well-known Düsseldorf Academy in 1855. The
Academy attracted many young American artists with its
high quality and rigidly structured training in landscape
painting. Haseltine returned to New York where he was
very successful. He finally settled in Rome in 1874 and
concentrated on picturesque landscapes that further
explored his fascination with shoreline views.

Haseltine visited Venice many times and often painted
its haze-enveloped *palazzi,* canals, and gondolas. This
painting depicts a view across the lagoon, or the Grand
Canal, toward the prominent bell tower on San Marco
Square. Influenced by American Luminism and French
Impressionism, Haseltine's brushstrokes became looser
and his palette lightened. These influences can be seen
in the way that light, color, and space prevail over the
subject and setting of the painting.

69

Edmund Darch Lewis, American, 1835–1910
Mount Washington, New Hampshire, 1865
Oil on canvas, 51⁷/₈ x 90¹/₂
Signed and dated lower left: *Edmund D. Lewis 1865*
Morton R. Hirschberg Memorial Fund

AP 1990.17.1

Born and educated in Philadelphia, Edmund Darch
Lewis studied painting for only a short time before he
began exhibiting at the Pennsylvania Academy of the
Fine Arts and later at the National Academy of Design in
New York. He quickly became one of the most popular
painters in Philadelphia, specializing in landscapes and
marine scenes of New England.

This monumental painting highlighting Mount
Washington in north central New Hampshire is sublime
and picturesque in its grandeur. The placid, timeless
scene depicts the majesty and power of nature and
evokes the doctrine of Manifest Destiny that motivated
settlers to explore America's frontiers. The heroic
landscape appears virtually unspoiled by human
encroachment, yet signs of taming the wilderness are
evident in the well-traveled path, the cleared land,
the grazing cows, and the inclusion of two fishermen.
Lewis followed the nineteenth-century formula for
landscapes by depicting a foreground, middleground,
and background receding into infinity. The preparatory
sketch done on site for this panoramic view can be
found in the Edmund Darch Lewis Sketchbook
Collection at The Athenaeum in Philadelphia.

70

Winslow Homer, American, 1836–1910
Waiting for a Bite, 1874
Oil on canvas, 11$^{15}/_{16}$ x 20$^1/_8$
Signed and dated lower left: *Winslow Homer 1874*
Bequest of Ninah M. H. Cummer

C 119.1

This small painting by Winslow Homer captures two boys
perched on a huge tree trunk that has fallen into a river.
One of the boys holds a fishing pole, the other looks on
intently. In the decade following the Civil War
(1861–1865), Homer, moved by the atrocities of the
battlefields, often turned to children as a theme in his art.
The innocence of childhood and the tranquility of fishing,
the artist's favorite pastime, became symbols of hope and
renewal for the nation following the painfully divisive
conflict. Homer also published this scene as a wood
engraving in *Harper's Weekly* (August 22, 1874).
The magazine illustration is identical to the Cummer's
painting, with two exceptions. In the illustration Homer
added a third boy with a fishing pole. Another contrast
between the pictures can be noted in the treatment of the
backgrounds. Whereas the wood engraving shows a lush
landscape of trees and bushes, the Cummer painting shows
a desolate plane with broken trees and burned grass,
a possible reminder of the devastating effects of war.

Homer was born in Boston in 1836, the son of an
established New England family. He was largely self-
taught and trained as an illustrator for various Boston
magazines. He covered the Civil War as an illustrator for
Harper's Weekly. Early in his career his great interest was
the naturalistic representation of scenes of American
life. After settling in Prout's Neck, Maine, in 1883, he
painted marine scenes depicting the struggle
of man with the forces of nature.

71

Winslow Homer, American, 1836–1910
The White Rowboat, St. Johns River, 1890
Watercolor on paper, 14 x 20
Signed and dated lower right: *Homer 1890*
Bequest of Ninah M. H. Cummer

C 154.1

Winslow Homer was one of the first American painters
to liberate watercolor from being simply a tinted
drawing and to develop it as an independent medium.
Especially in his later watercolors, Homer attained his
purest artistic values through his painterly handling and
use of saturated colors. His watercolors expressed a
poetic vision not often found in his oil paintings.

Late in his career, Homer, an avowed sportsman, took
fishing vacations to various places. In the spring of 1890
he visited the St. Johns River in Florida. The landscape
stimulated in Homer a more spontaneous expression
and pure visual sensation of nature. He painted scenes
on the spot with a deft, fluid brush in full-bodied color.
In this work, one of forty known from his various Florida
visits, Homer simply and directly portrayed Florida
topography as a vast expanse of river and marshes,
punctuated by four swaying palm trees. Homer merged
the epic with the mundane as he placed the stark white
rowboat and three fishermen in this solitary habitat. The
towering, indigenous palm trees stand as testaments to
the dominance of nature over man.

72

Thomas Moran, American, 1837–1926
Ponce de León in Florida, 1877–78
Oil on canvas, 64³/₄ x 115⁷/₈
Signed and dated lower left: *T Moran 1878*

Acquired for the people of Florida by the Frederick H. Schultz family & NationsBank, Inc.
Additional funding provided by the Cummer Council

AP 1996.2.1

American printmaker, illustrator, and painter, Thomas Moran became renowned for his grand, epic landscape paintings of the American West. He traveled to Europe throughout his career, and in the 1870s and 1880s, Moran also traveled to the frontiers of the western United States and to Florida. During these sojourns, he made hundreds of sketches and watercolors, which he turned into illustrations for popular magazines and finished paintings on canvas.

Moran painted this work of early Florida history to hang behind the Speaker's chair in the House of Representatives in Washington, D.C. It was to accompany his two other monumental western frontier landscapes that hung in the U.S. Senate chamber. The painting depicts the Spanish conquistador Juan Ponce de León (c. 1474–1521) in the company of native Floridians. Ponce de León had sailed up the uncharted coast of eastern Florida in search of the mythic "fountain of youth." He named the new land *La Florida* for the abundance of flowers he saw when he arrived during the Easter season, or *Pascua florida*, meaning "flowery Easter."

Moran was familiar with the western Plains Indians and depicted them in the painting instead of the very distinctly different Timucuan people inhabiting Florida at the time of Ponce de León's arrival. While Moran's vision of history is romanticized, his depiction of the Florida landscape is more accurate in the rendering of the clearing surrounded by palms, palmettos, and live oaks covered in Spanish moss and indigenous vines.

73

Mary Cassatt, American, 1844–1926
Simone in a Large Plumed Hat, c. 1903
Pastel counterproof, 26 x 21
Museum purchase with funds provided by the Mae W.
Schultz Acquisition Endowment & the Cummer Council

AP 1992.8.1

The daughter of a wealthy family from Pennsylvania,
Mary Cassatt received her initial artistic training at the
Pennsylvania Academy of the Fine Arts. Against her
family's wishes, she moved to Paris where she remained
as an expatriate artist for more than forty years. By the
age of twenty-eight, Cassatt's work had been accepted to
the Paris Salon. Cassatt exhibited with the Impressionist
group four times between the years of 1877 and 1886,
the only American artist ever to be invited to do so.
Throughout her highly successful career, Cassatt
transcended traditional expectations for women.

Domestic scenes of upper-class Parisian mothers and
children comprise only one-third of Cassatt's oeuvre,
but form the basis for her continued popularity.
This sentimental image of a young girl holding a dog is
characteristic of Cassatt's mature Impressionistic style.
The composition is tightly cropped and the sitter is
pushed to the front of the picture plane. Such simple,
graceful compositions were greatly influenced by her
fascination with Japanese woodblock prints. Cassatt was
very adept at the medium of pastel and took advantage of
its spontaneity and subtle variations in color and texture.
Created by pressing a damp piece of paper against a
pastel drawing, this counterproof exhibits the muted,
highly atmospheric effects typical of Cassatt's work.

74

John Singer Sargent, American, 1856–1925
In the Alps, 1911
Oil on canvas, 20 x 28¹/₁₆
Signed lower right: *John S. Sargent*
Museum purchase with Council funds

AP 1990.20.1

John Singer Sargent was born in Florence, Italy, of well-to-do American parents. The family moved with the seasons between Rome, the French Riviera, the Swiss Alps, Germany, Spain, and London. He spoke of himself as "an American born in Italy, educated in France, who looks like a German, speaks like an Englishman and who paints like a Spaniard." Sargent received strict academic training as an artist, but his teachers encouraged him to execute his work with immediacy and rapidity and disapproved of any re-working.

Sargent's name is synonymous with elegant, dynamically executed portraits of affluent members of society. Portraiture was his springboard to fame, but he also excelled in painting large murals for Harvard University and the Boston Museum of Fine Arts. This joyous painting, very expressive in style, is notable for its quick and dynamic brushwork. On close inspection, the thick impasto becomes clearly visible, giving a rich texture to the painting. The sky, clouds, rocks, and alpine flowers fill this canvas, which Sargent painted during one of his sojourns in the Simplon Pass in the Oberland Alps of Switzerland. Imbued with enviable vigor, this work demonstrates the enjoyable expression of an inveterate sketcher, interested in landscape in full, direct sunlight.

75

Frederick Childe Hassam, American, 1859–1935
Afternoon in Pont-Aven, Brittany, 1897
Oil on canvas, 19³/₄ x 24¹/₁₆
Signed and dated lower left: *Childe Hassam 1897*
Bequest of Ninah M. H. Cummer

C 162.1

Childe Hassam is the painter most closely identified with
the development of American Impressionism. He broke
away from the conservative artistic establishment in
1897 and became intensely interested in French painting. Hassam was attracted to the French Impressionists'
commitment to outdoor painting and use of vivid colors.
In this work, his technique has evolved toward the
broken brushwork and radical effects of light and color
of the new style without slavishly surrendering to it. As
one critic wrote early in the twentieth century, "Hassam
saw the wisdom in French Impressionism. But these
things opened his eyes rather than governed his brush."

"I believe the man who will go down in posterity is the
man who paints his own time and the scenes of every-
day life around him.... There is nothing so interesting to
me as people," said Hassam in the October 1892 issue of
Art Amateur. The afternoon captured in this painting
shows a small group of Breton peasants dressed in their
Sunday best, watching a group of geese parading on a
street near the local church. Pont-Aven was a well-
known artists' colony on the northwest coast of France,
admired for the rugged terrain surrounding the village
and its proximity to the tempestuous English Channel.

76

Robert Henri, American, 1865–1929
Guide to Croaghan, 1913
Oil on canvas, 41³/₁₆ x 33¹/₁₆
Signed lower right: *Robert Henri*
Museum purchase with Council funds

AP 1976.1.1

Robert Henri, born Robert Henry Cozad, was raised in a
small town in Nebraska. After his father murdered a
cattleman, the Cozad family fled their frontier home for
Atlantic City and changed their names. Henri received his
first formal art training at the Pennsylvania Academy of
the Fine Arts and eventually studied in Paris under the
tutelage of William Bouguereau (1825–1905). Upon his
return to Philadelphia, Henri rejected the sentimentality of
French academic painting for contemporary scenes of
urban life in America. The influential group of painters
who followed Henri was dubbed the Ashcan School, a
derogatory name referring to what critics called the "ugly"
and "unappealing" subject matter of their work. As both a
teacher and a painter, Henri championed a form of social
realism that influenced generations of American artists.

Henri became best known for his forceful portraits of
everyday people. He applied his dark palette and bold
brushwork to scenes of the city and portraits of children,
workers, and the downtrodden. Believing in the
supremacy of the individual, Henri strove to capture the
character of each sitter. This portrait depicts Brian
O'Malley, the guide who escorted Henri and his wife to
the cliffs of Croaghan in Ireland. The unidealized
characteristics of this man are evident in his timeworn
face, bright eyes, ruddy complexion, and expressive
hands. Henri spent the last years of his life immersed in
the traditional culture and unspoiled landscape of
the Irish coast.

77

William Glackens, American, 1870–1938
The Lake, 1913–18
Oil on canvas, 25 x 30
Museum purchase with Council funds

AP 1987.2.1

A native of Philadelphia, William Glackens began his artistic career as a newspaper illustrator. In 1891, he enrolled in evening classes at the Pennsylvania Academy of the Fine Arts and met Robert Henri (1865–1929), who encouraged Glackens to paint. After the National Academy of Design rejected Glackens's work in 1907, he joined Henri and six others to establish a group of artists known as the Eight. Derisively referred to as the Ashcan School by contemporary critics, the Eight were noted for their images depicting the reality of life in industrialized surroundings.

Glackens traveled to France several times throughout his career. Significantly influenced by the works of the French Impressionists after a visit in 1912, Glackens shifted his focus from gritty urban scenes to images of middle-class leisure. This painting shows a lake in the White Mountains near Conway, New Hampshire, where the Glackens family spent several summers. The brilliant palette, tilted perspective, and loose brushstrokes found in this scene of languid boaters reflect the artist's assimilation of the Impressionist style. The patterning in the water and heavy applications of paint create a dynamic, energized composition.

78

Frederick Carl Frieseke, American, 1874–1939
Before Her Appearance, 1913
Oil on canvas, 51¼ x 51¼
Signed and dated lower left: *F.C. Frieseke 1913*
Museum purchase with Council funds

AP 1985.2.1

Applying the last bit of ardent rouge to her lips before
going on stage, a dancer sits on a stool in her dressing
room, looking at herself in the mirror. This intimate
scene was captured by the American Impressionist artist
Frederick Carl Frieseke with a very tender, almost
monochromatic palette of pink, pale blue, marble white,
and an occasional patch of yellow.

Born in Ossowo, Michigan of German ancestry, Frieseke
studied painting in Chicago and Paris. He spent most of
his adult life in Europe and explained, "I stay on here,
because I am more free and there are not the Puritanical
restrictions which prevail in America.... I can paint a
nude in my garden or down by the fish pond and not be
run out of town."

This painting was created while Frieseke spent the
winter of 1912 on Corsica, an island off the Italian coast.
He rented a house and garden there and sent for his
favorite model Marcelle, who poses as the dancer in this
painting. He wrote to an art dealer that he had nothing
prepared for the upcoming Paris Salon exhibition.
Nevertheless, Frieseke was able to complete six
canvases that winter for inclusion in the Salon that
spring. *Before Her Appearance* was among them and was
very well received. It was bought by Mrs. Gertrude
Whitney Vanderbilt for her private collection.

79

Richard Emil Miller, American, 1875–1943
Café L'Avenue, Paris, c. 1906–10
Oil on canvas, 45⁷/₁₆ x 57 ⁵/₈
Signed lower left: *R.E. Miller*
Museum purchase with Council funds

AP 1985.1.1

Richard Emil Miller was born in St. Louis, Missouri, and left as a young man for Paris to study on a scholarship. A resident in France for close to twenty years, Miller was an active member of the American group of expatriate artists who converged on Giverny to be near the famous painter Claude Monet (1840–1926). On his return to the United States, Miller settled briefly in Pasadena, California, before establishing his studio in Provincetown, Massachusetts. Miller was much acclaimed in his lifetime, receiving the Legion of Honor medal from the French government and the Potter Palmer gold medal from the Art Institute of Chicago. He died while wintering in St. Augustine, Florida.

Café scenes were one of Miller's favorite subjects. In 1912, he stated his creative credo, "Art's mission is not literary, the telling of a story, but decorative, the conveying of a pleasant optical sensation." Miller painted this popular Parisian meeting place with evident gusto. Two elegant young women drinking an apéritif are seated at a small table listening to a piano, cello, and violin ensemble. To their right a waiter takes an order, while passers-by can be observed through the windows. Miller painted this moment with a keen eye for color, design, composition, and mood. The whole scene exudes an atmosphere of civility and good manners, a state of affairs to be shattered just a few years later by the outbreak of World War I.

80

Anna Hyatt Huntington, American, 1876–1973
Diana of the Hunt, 1922; recast 1960–61
Bronze, 98
Gift of Anna Hyatt Huntington

AG 1961.15.1

Anna Hyatt Huntington trained in New York at the Art Students League in 1895. After working with several prominent American sculptors, she traveled to France and Italy. She exhibited a large equestrian statue at the Paris Salon in 1910 and received an honorable mention. Hyatt Huntington was particularly well known for her accurate rendering of animal and human anatomy. Throughout her long career she received numerous commissions for sculptures and received awards including a Rodin Gold Medal in Philadelphia.
She was elected to the American Academy of Arts and Letters. The original cast of Hyatt Huntington's *Diana* was awarded a Saltus Medal for Merit by the National Academy of Design in New York in 1922.

In 1960, while the Cummer Museum of Art & Gardens was still under construction, Hyatt Huntington offered to have her sculpture of Diana recast so that it could be placed in the future gardens of the museum. The artist had a long history of installing her sculptures in gardens. She and her late husband Archer Huntington fully conceived and decorated Brookgreen Gardens, one of their estates in South Carolina.

Diana was the Roman goddess of women and patroness of the hunt, represented here by her hunting dog and bow. Her role as earth-bound huntress is complemented by her identity as the goddess of the moon, and Diana's placement in the Cummer gardens bridges these earthly and heavenly roles. Balanced atop an earthly globe, the lithe figure of the goddess stretches upward after shooting an arrow toward her celestial attribute, the moon.

81

Edmund William Greacen, American, 1877–1949
Brooklyn Bridge, East River, 1916
Oil on canvas, 30¹/₈ x 29⁷/₈
Signed lower left: *Edmund Greacen*
Gift of Mr. & Mrs. René Faure

AG 1972.2.1

This view of the Brooklyn Bridge was probably painted
from the roof of Edmund Greacen's building on East
18th Street, the first apartment building erected in all of
New York. With his use of broken brushwork and
sketchy atmospheric color, the artist captured several
aspects of the big city. He juxtaposed the gritty energetic
foreground of industrial buildings with the beautifully
subdued and suffused background of the East River and
the Brooklyn skyline.

Edmund Greacen studied painting at the Art Students
League in New York. Between 1906 and 1909 he lived in
Paris and Giverny studying the works of the French
Impressionists, particularly those of Claude Monet
(1840–1926). The admission of several of his paintings to
the Paris Salon attests to his early success. Greacen
returned to America and opened the first of two art schools
in New York and exerted great influence as a teacher.

82

Jonas Lie, American, 1880–1940
View of the Seine, 1909
Oil on canvas, 30⅛ x 40⅛
Signed and dated lower left:
Jonas Lie 1909/Jonas Lie
Museum purchase with Council funds

AP 1990.21.2

Jonas Lie portrays two highly characteristic bridges span-
ning the river Seine in Paris. Prominently represented is
the Pont des Arts, a cast-iron bridge exclusively used by
pedestrians. On this bridge one can see the stalls of the
bouquinistes, the Parisian booksellers who sell their
books, prints, and postcards from small, movable carts.
This trade is still plied along the banks of the Seine.
In the background looking eastward is the Pont-Neuf, a
stone bridge often painted by Impressionist artists, and
the western tip of the Ile de la Cité, the small island on
which the cathedral Notre-Dame de Paris is located.

Jonas Lie, son of a Norwegian father and American
mother, spent his formative years in Norway, Paris, and
New Jersey. He studied at the National Academy of
Design in New York and regularly returned to Paris to
maintain his international artistic contacts. Lie's series
of twelve paintings documenting the construction of the
Panama Canal is preserved in the Military Academy
at West Point.

Sir Jacob Epstein, American/English, 1880–1959
Seventh Portrait of Kathleen, 1948
Bronze, 27¼
Gift of The Honorable & Mrs. Bryan Simpson

AG 1978.1.1

The son of Polish immigrants, Jacob Epstein was born in New York and received his first artistic training at the Art Students League. The young artist worked a variety of jobs and made extra money selling his drawings of life on the Lower East Side. During a winter spent in a remote lake community in New Jersey, Epstein worked cutting ice. He said, "I felt here a full outlet for my energy, both physical and mental, that was far more satisfying to me than drawing." Epstein decided to become a sculptor and traveled to Paris to study at the Académie Julian. In 1905 he settled permanently in England. As a collector of non-Western sculpture, his work was heavily influenced by Assyrian, Indian, and African art. Epstein's critics found much of his large-scale sculpture controversial because of its often sensual nature, but the creation of smaller portrait busts brought him steady work throughout his career. Epstein received an honorary doctorate from Oxford University in 1953 and was knighted in 1954.

In 1921 Epstein met an art student named Kathleen Garman. After the death of his first wife in 1947, Epstein married Kathleen in 1955. Throughout their decades-long relationship, Kathleen served as an inspirational ideal of feminine beauty for the artist. Her unique facial features are emphasized through the contrast of light and dark in the bust. In the finished bronze, Kathleen's hands, hair, and face bear the marks made by Epstein's fingers and tools on the clay model he used to create the piece. The result is a lively, expressive portrait.

84

George Bellows, American, 1882–1925
Emma in an Orchard, 1916
Oil on canvas, 30⅛ x 38⅛
Signed lower left: *Geo. Bellows E.S.B.*
Museum purchase with Council funds

AP 1980.1.1

Born and raised in Ohio, George Bellows chose to
pursue a career in art over an offer to play professional
baseball for the Cincinnati Reds. Upon leaving Ohio
State University, Bellows moved to New York using
money he had earned selling his illustrations and
playing semi-professional ball. In New York Bellows
studied with Robert Henri (1865–1929), who became
both a mentor and admirer of the young artist. In 1908
at the age of twenty-six, Bellows became the youngest
member ever elected to the National Academy of Design
in New York. He achieved great success and popularity
as both an exhibiting artist and a teacher. Bellows
taught at the Art Students League in New York and the
School of the Art Institute of Chicago. Unfortunately,
Bellows's life and career were cut short when he died
from a ruptured appendix at the age of forty-two.

Bellows is best known for his energetic scenes of city
life, especially those of boxing matches. In sharp
contrast to these works, the paintings created during his
summers in Maine and Rhode Island depict a leisurely,
patrician world. In this painting, Bellows captures his
wife Emma bathed in the summer light of Camden,
Maine, a favorite vacation spot of the Bellows family.
Bold strokes of violet and green dance across the
surface of the canvas, infusing the work with a sense of
spontaneity. Emma appears as a vision of serenity
amidst the flurry of paint and color.

85

William Zorach, American, 1887–1966
Spirit of the Dance, 1932
Bronze, 77
Inscribed and dated: *Zorach 1932*
stamped: *3/6, Modern Art Foundry New York*
Morton R. Hirschberg Memorial Fund

AP 1990.21.1

William Zorach was born in Lithuania in 1889, but moved with his family to Cleveland, Ohio, when he was four. He first worked as a commercial artist in that city before receiving formal training as a painter in New York and Paris. He began carving wood in 1917, but devoted himself exclusively to sculpture in 1922. Zorach took great delight in finding unusual and exotic woods in order to experiment with their special characteristics such as grain, hardness, and color.

Zorach's *Spirit of the Dance* was selected by the Rockefeller family to be placed inside Radio City Music Hall in New York. Cast in the then ultra modern medium of aluminum, the monumental dancer taking a bow was completed in 1932. Considerable controversy developed over the nudity of the figure when the sculpture was first exhibited, and for some months the dancer disappeared from view. When the artist exhibited a clay model, however, it was so well received by art critics and the general public that the aluminum sculpture was returned to public view at Radio City Music Hall where it can still be seen. Zorach authorized an edition of six bronze casts of this sculpture.

86

Eugene Berman, American 1899–1972
Wreckage and Debris on the Beach, 1935
Oil on canvas, 32 x 23$\frac{1}{2}$
Signed and dated on verso:
E Berman, New York, 1935
Museum purchase

AP 1972.11.1

Eugene Berman was born in St. Petersburg, Russia, into
an established family of bankers and lawyers. His father
died when Berman was seven years old and his mother
remarried. His stepfather became responsible for the
boy's education and sent him to private schools in
Germany, Switzerland, and France. The family moved to
Paris in 1919 after the Bolshevik Revolution. At the
invitation of friends, the artist moved to the United
States in 1935 and became an American citizen. In 1956
he settled in Rome where he lived until his death.
Well known as a costume and set designer for the
Metropolitan Opera in New York, Berman was also an
accomplished easel painter.

The painting shows a beach masquerading as a waste-
land desert with mysteriously suggestive objects and
people. The empty sarcophagus in the right foreground,
the terracotta jug, and the flotsam and jetsam
characteristic of a beach after a storm, are crowded
together in the silent vastness of the empty landscape.
In the upper left-hand corner, a knotted rope dangles,
visually balancing the diagonal of the seesaw.
The seated muse, crawling man, and conversing couple
add a piquant accent to the visual, slightly surreal
composition. The painting's dream-like mystery is well
suited to interpretations of the subconscious.

87

John Steuart Curry, American, 1897–1946
Parade to War, Allegory, 1938
Oil on canvas, 40$^1/_{16}$ x 56$^1/_8$
Signed and dated lower right:
John Steuart Curry, 1938.
Gift of Barnett Banks, Inc.

AG 1991.4.1

John Steuart Curry enrolled in classes at the Kansas City
Art Institute while still a junior in high school in rural
Kansas. Initially he earned a living illustrating popular
stories of the Wild West. Curry entered the most productive and successful period of his career in the 1930s.
He taught at Cooper Union and the Art Students League
in New York. He also received mural commissions as
part of the Federal Art Project, which employed artists
after the Great Depression. Curry's public mural projects
concentrated on themes of religious intolerance, racial
discrimination, and social upheaval. In 1936 he was
appointed artist-in-residence within the College of
Agriculture at the University of Wisconsin, a post he
held until his death. Curry is identified with the
Regionalist movement through his depictions of the
history, people, and landscape of the American Midwest.

Parade to War, Allegory was painted in the wake of the
Great Depression and on the eve of World War II
(1939–1945). Curry turns the pageantry of a parade into
a scene of foreboding and dread, most obviously
disclosed in the skeletal faces of the young soldiers.
The panic and sorrow of the two women in the
foreground contrast with the hopeful innocence of the
central striding couple and the young boys gathering
streamers. Typical of Curry's work, this painting
represents the isolationist attitudes and growing
disillusionment expressed by an increasing number of
Americans in the late 1930s.

Thomas Hart Benton, American, 1889–1975
June Morning, 1945
Oil on masonite, 41⁷/₈ x 48¹/₁₆
Signed and dated lower right: *Benton 45*
Museum purchase with funds provided by the Cummer
Council, the Morton R. Hirschberg Memorial Fund, & the
Mae W. Schultz Acquisition Endowment

AP 1994.2.1

Thomas Hart Benton was born in the small Missouri
town of Neosho to a family of politicians. His father was
a congressman and his great uncle was the first United
States senator west of the Mississippi and the longest-
serving senator to date. Benton pursued an art career
despite the dissatisfaction of his family, first attending
the School of the Art Institute of Chicago and then
studying in Paris. His earliest works were explorations of
various modernist styles, but by the 1920s Benton began
to forge his strongly personal style, which is
characterized by grand compositions brimming with
curvilinear forms, realistic details, and intensified colors.

The central figure in the Regionalist movement, Benton
used his art to elevate the experiences of everyday
people and ordinary events. He discovered deeper
meaning in seemingly straightforward experiences in
the rural Midwest. Characteristic of Benton's mature
style, *June Morning* depicts a view from his mother's
house on Martha's Vineyard. In the foreground, the
vibrant, twining foliage parts to reveal their neighbor
Henry Look milking a cow. The Atlantic Ocean is visible
in the distance. Painted one month after Germany's
surrender in World War II, this work is Benton's patriotic
testament to the strength of the American spirit in the
face of the destructive powers of war. Henry Look
symbolizes Benton's vision of the American way of life,
and the departing storm clouds suggest the passing
threat of war. The cycle of life is represented by the
bountiful new growth that dominates the foreground
and the broken, dead tree in the distance.

89

Abraham Rattner, American, 1895–1978
Yellow Crucifixion, 1953
Oil on masonite, 45³/₄ x 35¹/₄
Signed and dated on verso: *Rattner 1953*
Gift of Genny, Clifford, & Robert Ayers in Memory of
Genevieve Schultz Ayers

AG 1987.7.1

Abraham Rattner was born in New York, the son of a
Russian rabbi. In 1917 he enrolled in the Pennsylvania
Academy of the Fine Arts, but soon left to serve as a
camouflage artist in France during World War I. In 1920
Rattner received a fellowship and moved to Paris. While
living there he was influenced by modern painting styles
and the simplified figurative forms found in earlier
Romanesque and Byzantine art. Soon after his return to
the United States in 1939, Rattner spent several months
touring the South by car with novelist Henry Miller,
whom he had met in Paris. During their excursion from
New York to Louisiana, they made a brief stop in
Jacksonville, Florida. The trip inspired Miller to write
The Air-Conditioned Nightmare.

Rattner's style of figurative expressionism combined
traditional themes with the formal elements of
Modernism. The theme of the crucifixion grew out
of Rattner's reaction to World War II. For Rattner,
the crucifixion became a symbol of man's condition.
He included himself in this spiritual examination when
he said, "It is myself that is on the cross, though I am
attempting to express a universal theme—man's
inhumanity to man." In *Yellow Crucifixion* Rattner
shatters and reassembles the image of a figure on
a golden cross. The brightly colored facets of thick
paint and the delineating black lines are reminiscent
of the Gothic stained glass windows Rattner admired
during a brief residence in Chartres, site of the
famous French cathedral.

90

Augusta Savage, American, 1892–1962
The Diving Boy, c. 1939
Bronze, 32½
Inscribed: *Augusta Savage*
Bequest of Ninah M. H. Cummer

C 602.1

Born in Green Cove Springs, Florida, the seventh of
fourteen children, Augusta Savage exhibited a talent and
interest in the arts at an early age. After a marriage that
left her widowed at the age of sixteen, Savage moved to
Jacksonville, Florida to earn a living sculpting portrait
busts of prominent African Americans. In 1921, she
moved to New York and enrolled in the Cooper Union.
She received many fellowships and awards, allowing
her to travel and study abroad. In 1932 Savage began a
notable teaching career with the founding of the Savage
School of Arts and Crafts in New York. As an important
figure in the Harlem Renaissance of the 1920s and
1930s, Savage worked with other important leaders,
writers, musicians, and artists to celebrate the contributions of African American culture to American society.
She overcame poverty, racism, and sexual
discrimination to become one of twentieth-century
America's most prolific and influential sculptors.
Because of her often difficult financial situation, Augusta
Savage's plaster originals were frequently destroyed
before she could afford to have them cast in bronze.

Augusta Savage visited Ninah Cummer at her Jacksonville
home in 1939 and presented *The Diving Boy* as a gift the
following year. Originally placed at one end of a reflecting
pond in Mrs. Cummer's Italian Garden, the sculpture is
typical of Savage's interest in combining realistic details
with psychologically penetrating expressiveness.

91

David Smith, American, 1906–1965
Ring-toothed Woman, 1950
Steel, 12
Incised: *Δ Σ, #2, 50*
Gift of Mr. Joseph Jeffers Dodge

AG 1998.1.1

Diminutive, standing only twelve inches high, this
enigmatic sculpture by David Smith has a grandeur all
its own. Its intriguing title begs the question of who or
what is a ring-toothed woman. Smith found his inspiration in disparate sources and created a suggestive form
that contains various layers of allusion. The sculpture's
central oval is adorned with teeth-like triangles, giving
the work a menacing presence. Smith made the original
sculpture in 1945 (now in the Hirshhorn Museum and
Sculpture Garden), but cast a second version in 1950,
which he presented as a wedding present to his friend,
Joseph J. Dodge (1917–1997). Dodge, a painter, art
historian, and former director of the Cummer Museum
of Art & Gardens, had befriended David Smith in 1941
when Smith was working as a machinist in Glen Falls,
New York. Dodge was curator at the local museum.

Smith initially trained as a painter and held a number of
summer jobs as a welder in a car factory. After seeing
photographs of modernist sculpture, he realized that his
welding skills could be put to use making sculpture.
During a Sunday afternoon walk on a navy pier in
Brooklyn, he spotted Terminal Iron Works, a commercial
welding firm. The next morning he walked in and was
met by the owner, a big Irishman, and proclaimed, "I'm
an artist, I have a welding outfit. I'd like to work here."
The man responded, "Hell! Yes. Move in." David Smith
started making sculpture then and there.

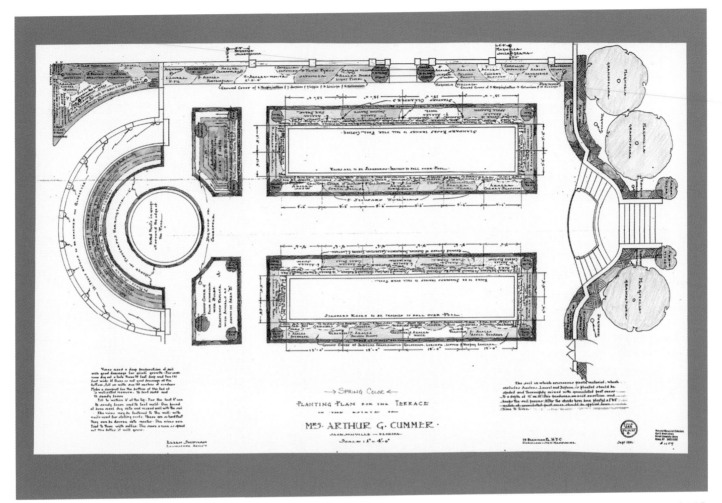

92

→ SPRING COLOR ←

PLANTING PLAN for the TERRACE

in the estate of

MRS. ARTHUR G. CUMMER.
JACKSONVILLE — FLORIDA.
Scale: 1" = 4'-0"

Stela of Iku and Mer-imat

Egyptian, Middle Kingdom, XI Dynasty, c. 2100 B.C.

Painted on limestone, 23¼ x 20 ⅝ x 5

Morton R. Hirschberg Memorial Fund

AP 1989.1.1

This stela depicts a nobleman named Iku and his wife, Mer-imat. One of the principal purposes of the stela is explained in the vertical inscription located in front of the striding Iku. This written "appeal to the living" asks those who pause in front of it to read the text aloud, providing the deceased with "a thousand of bread and beer, a thousand of beef and fowl, and of everything good, for the high official, the honored Iku." The text above Mer-imat's head describes her titles as "king's [ornament], priestess of Hathor, honored one, beautiful of ornament, overseer of oasis-dwellers." That Mer-imat's titles are significantly more elaborate than those of her husband suggests that Iku may have owed his noble position to their marriage. The wealth of the couple is underscored by their fine dress that includes intricately beaded wigs, jeweled collars, armlets, and anklets. Iku's staff and scepter are traditional symbols of position and authority.

This funerary stela is almost certainly from Naga-ed-Deir, a village in Upper Egypt on the bank of the river Nile. The stela closely resembles nearly one hundred relief carvings found in the offering chambers of tombs in the vast cemetery at Naga-ed-Deir. Despite its fragmentary condition, the expertly carved surface and the original polychrome are well preserved.

93

Attic Black-figure Amphora
Greek, c. 520–510 B.C.
Side A: Dionysos between dancing satyrs
Side B: Maenads
Terracotta, 16
Museum purchase

AP 1966.21.1

This amphora has scenes on two sides, one of which depicts Dionysos, the Greek god of wine, flanked by two dancing satyrs. Dressed in a long draped robe, Dionysos carries the identifying symbols of a large *kantharos*, or drinking vessel, and three sprigs of a grapevine. On the opposite side, five women are arranged in a lively procession. Two of the women carry *krotala*, or castanets, while the woman in the center holds tendrils of a grapevine. These women are most likely maenads, the female devotees of Dionysos. The images that decorate this piece relate directly to its function as a vessel for the storage of wine.

During the Archaic period, vase painting was a major pictorial art form, indicated by the proliferation of various vase shapes and known workshops from the late seventh century to the fifth century B.C. The amphora, a two-handled narrow-necked vase used for the storage and transport of liquid and food, was a favored shape. The Cummer example was executed using the black-figure technique, in which figures were painted with black slip and silhouetted against the light background of the natural red clay.

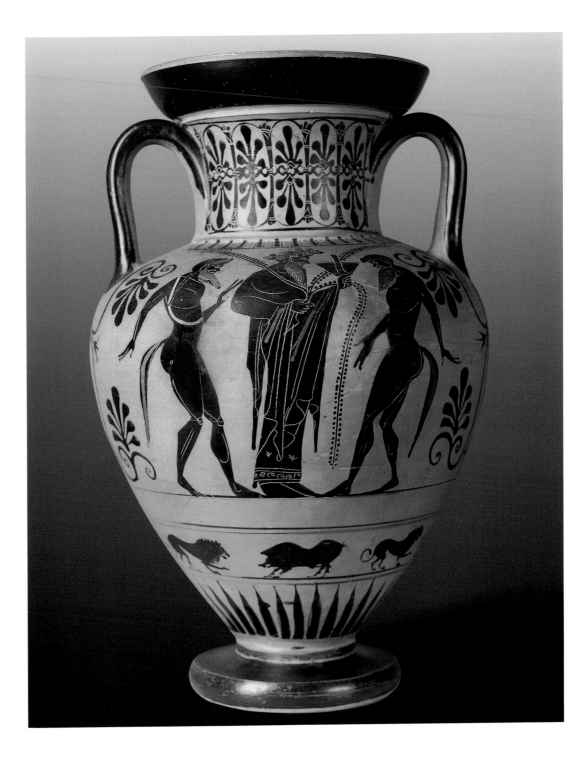

94

Attic Black-figure Kylix
Greek, c. 520–500 B.C.
Side: Youth riding a hippalektryon
Terracotta, 4" high, 8¹/₂" in diameter
Museum purchase

AP 1966.28.1

This kylix, or drinking cup, is one of about thirty vessels traditionally classified as the Group of Courting Cups. They are all eye cups of consistent shape, typified by a shallow bowl, plain lip, and a short, splayed foot. Appearing on both sides of the kylix, the eyes become part of a face when the cup is tipped to drink; the handles mimic ears, and the foot, a nose. The eyes may be merely a decorative element or may be apotropaic in nature, warding off evil and bad fortune. The majority of the courting cups, including this example, depict scenes of courtship between a man and boy on at least one side. This choice of subject seems fitting because of the cup's use at a *symposion*, an all-male gathering.

Also depicted on this kylix is a male youth riding a hippalektryon, a mythical creature, half horse and half rooster. Most hybrid creatures seem to have been introduced to Greek culture from the East, but the hippalektryon has no known prototype. The animal appears regularly on Attic vases from 550 to 500 B.C., but is scarcely mentioned by Greek writers of the day. It is mentioned once in Aristophanes's play, *The Frogs*, as "the tawny cock-horse" painted on ships, and once by Aeschylus, who claimed that by the late fifth century the average Athenian had never heard of such a creature.

95

Mirror
Etruscan, late 4th century B.C.
Bronze, 10³/₄" high, 5¹/₂" in diameter
Gift of Dr. M. Anwar Kamal

AG 1984.5.1

Etruscan civilization flourished in Italy from the ninth to
the first century B.C. when the Etruscans were
integrated into the Roman Empire. Little is known
about their origin, and their language is only partially
understood. Nevertheless, cultural achievements of the
Etruscans influenced Mediterranean cultures and played
an important role in the development of Roman society.
Among the Etruscan contributions traditionally
attributed to the Romans are the arch, the invention of
concrete, Roman numerals, and the toga.

The production of mirrors in Etruria, located in what is
now central Italy, began during the second half of the
sixth century B.C. Thus far, these luxury items have been
discovered in women's tombs only. The non-reflecting
or reverse side is often engraved with scenes of daily
Etruscan life and mythology. The Cummer mirror, cast in
one piece, is incised with a scene of adornment.
The woman is seated on a stool surrounded by items
related to her toilette. A winged hermaphrodite stands
poised to crown the woman with a wreath, while a bird
brings her a necklace in its beak. The seated woman has
been identified as Malavisch, the Etruscan name for a
figure associated with wedding rituals. Scenes of bridal
adornment are common on Etruscan mirrors, supporting
the idea that these objects were given as wedding gifts.

96

Mosaic with Mask of Silenus
Roman, 1st century A.D.
Stone tesserae and cement, 12¼ x 12¼ x 2½
Morton R. Hirschberg Memorial Fund

AP 1990.19.1

The technique of creating mosaics consists of embedding small pieces of colored stone, marble, or glass, called *tesserae*, into a base of cement or plaster. Mosaics were used as a durable alternative to floor coverings because of the relative permanence of these materials. The art of mosaic was developed extensively by the ancient Romans for decorating pavements. Mosaics were only one element in a unified decorative program that included wall frescoes, sculptures, furniture, and ornamental architectural elements.

Depictions of masks and masked figures appear in mosaics throughout the ancient Roman world. This mosaic is a mask of Silenus, a woodland deity associated with the Greek god Dionysos and the Greek theater. Silenus was the tutor of Dionysos and was reputed to possess great practical wisdom and the power of prophecy. He became the chief comic character of the satyr plays written by Greek tragedians. The mask depicts Silenus with a beard, snub nose, gaping mouth, grimacing brow, and wild gaze. His broad face is framed by a garland of leaves, a reference to the ivy sacred to Dionysos.

97

Johann Friedrich Böttger, German, 1682–1719
Vase and Lid, c. 1715
Porcelain, 9¹/₂
Gift of Ms. Constance I. & Mr. Ralph H. Wark

AG 1965.36.25

Considered so precious it was referred to as "white gold," porcelain was a highly prized item in European court society in the eighteenth and nineteenth centuries. Porcelain manufacture was a carefully guarded secret of the Orient. After reports of the quality and luminosity of Chinese porcelain reached Europe, efforts were made to replicate the East Asian product. The story of the introduction of porcelain into Europe is fraught with tales of alchemy, arcane formulae, closely guarded secrets, industrial espionage, and betrayal. The major obstacle was finding the right mix of kaolin, quartz, and feldspar to produce "true" or hard-paste porcelain. Using a combination of alchemy, hard work, and hubris, a young man working in Meissen, a small town near Dresden, Germany, produced the first porcelain made in Europe after his attempts to make gold had failed.

In 1710 the Royal Saxon Porcelain Manufacture was established in Albrechtsburg Castle in Meissen under the patronage of Augustus the Strong, Elector of Saxony and King of Poland (1670–1733), a passionate collector of Chinese porcelain objects. The factory flourished and dominated the European market until the Prussian occupation of the city in 1756. The success of the Meissen factory was directly related to the mining and smelting industries in the nearby Erz Mountains. Engineers and chemists active there provided the necessary technical and scientific basis for a systematic search for the secret of producing hard-paste porcelain. Three men were instrumental in the invention and development of early Meissen porcelain manufacture: Johann Friedrich Böttger (1682–1719), first manager of the porcelain studio, Johann Gregor Höroldt (1696–1755), a gifted decorator, and Johann Joachim Kändler (1706–1775), sculptor and modeler of figurines.

Böttger had attracted the attention of Augustus the Strong through his promising experiments of making gold by means of alchemy. Working under close guard, Böttger failed to produce gold and was transferred to the porcelain operation. In 1708, under Böttger's direction, a red stoneware was successfully produced. It was so hard that it could be cut and polished much like semiprecious stone. It was not until 1715, however, that true porcelain was made in Meissen. Böttger and his staff were virtually held prisoners in the Albrechtsburg Castle because Augustus did not want the *arcanum,* or secret of making porcelain, disclosed. In 1719 at the age of thirty-seven, Böttger died. A year later a young miniature painter named Johann Georg Höroldt joined the factory. Porcelain created under his supervision is noted for its high quality of painting and coloring. Particularly prized are the pieces with oriental decoration such as ceramics in the Kakiemon style, named after the famous potter family from the Arati province in Japan.

In 1723 the Meissen factory introduced the use of a potter's mark on its porcelain. The first one was *KPM (Königliche Porzellan Manufaktur)*, followed a year later by the famous crossed swords taken from the coat of arms of Augustus the Strong. Pieces intended for personal use by the Elector and King were marked *AR (Augustus Rex)*. In 1731 Johann Joachim Kändler joined the factory as a modeler. Working in close association with Count Heinrich von Brühl, director of the factory, the emphasis shifted to sculpted forms such as figures of animals and birds, chandeliers, and the famous Dresden figures, porcelain pieces of mythological or allegorical characters.

The Ralph H. and Constance I. Wark Collection of early Meissen porcelain is one of the three finest and most comprehensive collections in the world. Ralph Wark (1902–1987) bought his first Meissen piece in 1922, and over the next sixty years acquired more than seven hundred objects. Before World War II, Mr. Wark was a representative of the National Cash Register Corporation in Europe and traveled extensively on the Continent. At various times, he lived in Hamburg, Paris, London, and Berlin. Ralph Wark and his sister Constance, residents of St. Augustine, donated this unique collection to the Cummer in 1965. The entire collection has been published in a special catalogue entitled *The Wark Collection Early Meissen Porcelain* (Cummer Museum of Art & Gardens, 1984).

Martin Schnell, German, active 1712–c. 1735
Dinner plate, c. 1730
Porcelain, 9 ⁷⁄₈
Gift of Ms. Constance I. & Mr. Ralph H. Wark

AG 2000.2.13

Johann Joachim Kändler, German, 1707–1775
Liqueur Barrel and Stand c. 1740
Porcelain, 16³/₈
Gift of Ms. Constance I. & Mr. Ralph H. Wark

AG 1967.13.10

The Eugène Louis Charvot Collection

Eugène Louis Charvot, French, 1847–1924
Peasant Girl Going Fishing, small version, 1904
Etching, dry point, watercolor, gouache and pencil
on paper, single state, 3 x 4
Signed lower left: *E Charvot*
Gift of Mrs. Yvonne Charvot Barnett in memory of
her father Eugène Louis Charvot

AG 1999.5.20

(opposite)
View of rue El-Alfahouine, 1889
Oil on canvas, 47 x 30³/₄
Signed and dated lower left: *Charvot. 1889*
Gift of Mrs. Yvonne Charvot Barnett in memory of her
father Eugène Louis Charvot

AG 1999.5.3

Eugène Louis Charvot was born in Moulins in central France. He studied medicine, became a doctor, and embarked on a long career in the French army. He was stationed in Tunisia, Algeria, Switzerland, and a number of locations in France. While stationed in Paris between 1871 and 1873, Charvot studied painting with Félix-Henri Giacomotti (1828–1909) and Léon-Joseph-Florentin Bonnat (1834–1923). Charvot exhibited landscapes at the Paris Salon in 1876 and later years and contributed paintings to annual exhibitions in the city of his birth. Despite early successes with landscapes and genre scenes from the Middle East, Charvot found his true artistic calling when he discovered etching in 1901. Over the next ten years he produced more than fifty small, delicately executed plates, which featured mostly landscapes, scenes of laboring peasants, and views of quaint French villages. He frequently entered the annual Salons and his etchings received numerous awards, particularly from the *Société des Aquafortistes,* of which he was elected president. The Charvot Collection is comprised of 19 paintings, 202 works on paper, and associated archival materials. Research on the collection is continuing and will be presented in special exhibitions and publications.

James McBey, American, 1883–1959
The Mirage, 1925
Etching on paper, 10^{15}/$_{16}$ x 17
Signed lower right: *James McBey.*
Gift of Mrs. James McBey

AG 1961.1.119

James McBey was born near the Scottish town of Aberdeen. He worked in banking until the age of twenty-seven, before devoting himself full-time to art. In 1911, McBey left Scotland for London, beginning a lifetime of travel that took him to Holland, France, Spain, Morocco, Italy, and America. He was appointed as an artist to the British Expeditionary Force in Egypt during World War I and created boldly realized visual documents of the sights and people of this desert kingdom. During a visit to the United States, McBey and his wife could not return to Europe because of the outbreak of World War II. He became an American citizen in 1942 and enjoyed a series of successful exhibitions in New York. Following the war, he settled in Morocco where he continued working on his drawings, prints, and watercolors until his death.

McBey was an accomplished draftsman and print-maker. In this panoramic view of Venice, McBey uses his strongly developed observational skills to reveal the details of the slowly moving sailboat and the ghostly skyline. McBey is able to achieve both architectural precision and atmospheric spaciousness with the fewest possible marks. This work is characteristic of his poetic, intimate views of historic cities and exotic destinations.

The Cummer is home to one of the largest collections of McBey's work outside of his native Scotland. Given to the museum by the artist's widow, the collection contains more than 140 works of art and includes etchings from every stage of his career as well as several watercolors.

103

Joseph Jeffers Dodge, American, 1917–1997
The Artist and His Muse, 1992
Oil on canvas, 36 x 36
Signed and dated lower left: *J. Dodge 92*
Gift of Mr. Joseph Jeffers Dodge

AG 1996.2.60

Joseph Jeffers Dodge was trained as an art historian and museum administrator at Harvard University before accepting his first job as curator of the Hyde Collection in Glen Falls, New York. At the same time, he began actively painting and exhibiting his work. In 1962 Dodge was invited to take the director's position at the Cummer Museum of Art & Gardens, a job he held for 10 years before making a full-time commitment to painting. The Dodge Collection was bequeathed to the museum in 1997. Constituting a comprehensive survey of the artist's development, the collection consists of 48 paintings, 50 drawings, photographs, and journals.

In a 1983 interview in *American Artist*, Dodge said that his career as a museum director was " ... an ideal thing. I could fulfill my fantasies with somebody else's money and see the results.... I still go to sleep at night and instead of counting sheep, I arrange a room with some kind of ideal collection of art. That's my thing." When asked if he would include his own work in his ideal collection, Dodge smiled enigmatically and then said, "I tend to paint the kind of pictures that I would want to buy if somebody else painted them." Dodge's paintings are carefully rendered depictions of people and places. "I want to make the painting specific enough so that it looks convincing," he said in the same interview, "but I am not a Photo-Realist. It's always an imaginary idea, a fantasy world that I try to make look real."

104

Tsukioka Yoshitoshi, Japanese, 1839–1892
*100 Views of the Moon, # 9, A Moonlight Scouting
Patrol: Saito Toshimitsu,* 1885
Woodblock print on paper published by Akiyama
Takeyemon, 14¹/₈ x 9¹⁵/₁₆
The Dennis C. Hayes collection

AG 1998.4.56

An important collection of 190 Japanese woodblock prints entered the Cummer's permanent collection in 1998, a gift of Mr. Dennis C. Hayes of Atlanta. The collection shows the evolution of woodblock prints from the renowned artist Katsushika Hokusai (1760–1849) to the twentieth-century artist Kawase (1883–1957). The collection is particularly strong in nineteenth-century examples of *ukiyo-e* woodcuts, or images of the floating world that were popular during the Meiji era (1868–1912).

Three artists are represented by more than forty prints each in the Hayes collection. Ando Hiroshighe (1797–1858), the son of a samurai, was a prolific master of the full-color landscape print. He made a journey in 1832 from Edo (Tokyo) to Kyoto along the 300-mile Tokaido highway, which inspired a series of prints called *Fifty-three Stations of the Tokaido.* These prints, thirteen of which are represented in the Cummer collection, excel in their keen observation and insight into nature. Toyahara Chikanobu (1838–1912), another artist whose

art is well represented, is particularly known for his series *The Court Ladies of the Chiyode Castle* (1895), a delightful portfolio of female portraits.

The third artist, Tsukioka Yoshitoshi, initially specialized in illustrations of current events for newspapers and magazines. His woodcuts were created for the increasingly profitable market for scenes of horror and the grotesque because of a declining interest in *ukiyo-e* prints. Radical changes in Japan brought about by western influences caused Yoshitoshi to suffer a nervous breakdown in 1872. A year later, he resumed his work and adopted the artist's name of Taiso Yoshitoshi. He is best known for his series of *100 Aspects of the Moon,* forty-seven of which are in the Hayes Collection at the Cummer. A strong foreshortening, sharp diagonal perspective, and aggressive cropping of the image characterize his mature style, evident in this portrayal of the ill-fated warrior Toshimitsu, shown in full armor preparing for battle.

Index

Concept of the catalogue	Kym Staiff, DOC design consulting.
Text edited by	Jeannie Theriault
Graphic design, typesetting, composition & photo work	Kym Staiff and Pierre–Yves Gadina DOC design consulting Vers le lac — 1813 St–Saphorin — Switzerland
Photography	Superstock, Inc. Thomas Hager (Garden Photos)
Photolithography and printing	Stamperia Artistica Nazionale Corso Siracusa 37 — 10136 Torino — Italy *Shipman Garden Plan* scanned by NGI Color Works, Jacksonville — FL
Typefaces, paper & print run	Composed in ITC Leawood and Helvetica. 5100 copies on 170 gm^2 Gardamat

ISBN 0-915135-10-8
Printed in Italy

Cummer Museum of Art & Gardens
829 Riverside Avenue
Jacksonville, FL 32204
www.cummer.org